Mexican Heritage Cookbook

Complemented With Wine

Mexican Heritage Cookbook

Complemented With Wine

Shelia Chávez

Westport Publishers Inc.

Kansas City, Missouri

Illustrations by: Roberta Hammer

Cover design by: Noelle Kaplan, finedesign

ISBN 0-933701-50-0

Library of Congress Number: 91-50002

To order additional copies, send check for $9.95 plus $3.00 shipping and handling fee (per copy) to Westport Publishers, Inc. 4050 Pennsylvania, Kansas City, Missouri 64111. For credit card orders, please call (816) 756-1490.

Printed in the United States of America

For
Arturo, Mi Amor
My two sons, Arturito and Mundito

CONTENTS

Preface xi
Acknowledgments xiii
Plan of This Book xiv
Mexican Cuisine and Wine 1
Characteristics of Selected Wines 2
How to Taste Wine 5
Some Mexican Cooking Terms 6
APPETIZERS 11
Shrimp Appetizer 13
Empanaditas 14
Guacamole 15
Little Meatballs 16
Sour Cream Dip with Jalapeños 17
Martha's Chicken Salad 18
Flutes 19
Little Tacos 19
Mexican Sandwich 20
SOUPS 21
Soup Mexican Style 23
Mexican Rice 24
Vermicelli Soup 25
Pork Stew 26
Pork Soup 28
Mostaccioli Soup 30
MEATS AND BARBECUES 31
Grilled Meat 34
Grandmother's Pot Roast 35
Beefsteak Mexican Style 36
Meat with Potatoes and Carrots 37

Meat Balls 38

Arturo's Meat in Red Chile Sauce 40

Meat in Red Chile Sauce 42

Peppers and Onions with Meat 43

Mexican Lasagne 44

Lety's Meatloaf 45

Mexican Stew 46

Mother's Taco Buffet 48

Breaded Steak 50

Loin of Pork in Green Chile Sauce 51

Pork with Tomatoes 52

Tender Pork Bits 53

Rice with Chicken 54

Mexican Chicken 55

Mexican Stuffed Chicken 56

EGGS 57

Chorizo with Eggs 59

Mexican Omelet 60

Arturo's Eggs 60

Eggs with Tortillas 61

Mexican Scrambled Eggs 62

CORN AND WHEAT 63

Enchiladas .65

Tacos 65

Tortillas 66

Burritos 67

Empanadas .68

Tortillas with Cheese 69

Potato Tacos 70

Crisp Fried Tortillas 71

Paula's Enchiladas and Sauce 72

Paula's Small Corn Tortillas 74

Martha's Tamales 76

Martha's Tamale Sauce 78
Elena's Tamale Filling 80
SAUCES 81
Chávez Special Salsa 83
Paula's Mole 84
Fresh Tomato Salsa 86
Red Chile Sauce 86
Piquín Sauce 87
Gera's Tomatíllo Sauce 88
VEGETABLES AND SALADS 89
Avocado Salad 91
Enchilada Salad 92
Mama's Macaroni Salad 93
Potato Salad 94
Cauliflower 95
Potatoes in Hot Sauce 96
Little Potato Cakes 97
Stuffed Chiles 98
Light Tomato Sauce 99
Comadre Celia's Stuffed Chiles 100
Beans 101
Prickly Pears 102
Cactus Leaves 102
BEVERAGES AND DESSERTS 103
Blue Moon Margaritas 105
Sangria 105
Banana Breakfast 106
Rice Pudding 107
Sweet Potatoes Mexican Style 108
Bread Pudding 109
Custard 110
Tropical Fruit Plate with Cheese 111
Filled Cookies 112

Sandra Maine's Pound Cake 113

Grandmother's Elegant Lemon Cake 114

Pecan or Pine Nut Bread 115

Tea Cakes 116

Dessert Turnovers 117

Mexican Doughnuts 118

Jell-O with Eggnog 119

SAMPLE MENUS 121

Preface

This is my Gringo's guide to Mexican cooking—the lessons I learned about how a "gringo" wife should cook for a Mexican husband! For me, romance and Mexican cooking go hand in hand, for I interrupted my college education to marry Arturo Chávez, a proud native of Celaya, México, and now long-time vineyard manager of the famed century old Wente Bros. wineries of Livermore, California.

That explains how I came to live on the beautiful old Wente estate and in the very old and beautiful home where the Wente brothers were born and raised. Since my marriage in 1970—a year after meeting Arturo, who was himself only 20 when he came to this country, I have been constantly in the kitchen, where I cook for Arturo and my two sons, Arthur John, now in college, and his younger brother, Edmund.

Marriage to a Mexican brings many difficulties to a new "gringo" bride. At first I knew nothing of Mexican cooking. Arturo and I cooked all meals together for the first year. Later on, as family and friends visited, I would watch and learn. Paula, Arturo's mother, and many Mexicans and other friends taught me their secrets, handed down from mother to daughter. Gradually, I learned that there are many variations upon the same themes, and that the test of proficiency is one's skill at improvisation.

Although you are free to spend as much as you like for more expensive ingredients, in the beginning I had to be very frugal, so you'll find that these are authentic, low-budget recipes. Tenderized round steak, for example, can be substituted for sirloin steak in many of the meat recipes; and many of my meatless recipes can be prepared and served as whole meals.

I have given you substitutes to choose from if you don't care for cleaning and grinding dry chiles. Notice that I sometimes combine the dry chiles with an excellent chile sauce so as to get all the flavor possible for a good dish. Chiles are a necessary part of Mexican cooking, but hotness does not determine the character

of genuine Mexican cooking. A mole sauce, or even a table salsa, whether very hot and spicy or mild, can be equally delicious.

You may find a Mexican grocery in your own community, and many other groceries often have Mexican sections where seasonings are available. Use these, because American seasonings—orégano, for example—are definitely different. Mexican orégano is less pungent than ours, with a decidedly different flavor. Our cinnamon sticks are quite hard, while the Mexican are soft and breakable. Some chiles may be hard to find, making substitution necessary. But remember to be cautious when adding new chiles. You can always add more chiles as you go along, but it's hard to take away the hotness after it's there!

Chiles are very hot whether fresh, canned, or dried. You may want to use gloves while cleaning or slicing chiles!

Many recipes can be served with American as well as Mexican food. For example, my simple roast beef recipe can be served with either rice or beans, or can be used to make tacos or burritos.

Tortillas are a must at almost every meal. For many years I have prepared homemade corn and flour tortillas. I have found fresh corn tortillas in nearby stores, but my family still prefers thicker, homemade flour tortillas, so I buy flour, masa trigo (flour tortilla mix), to which I just add water.

The blender is a handy kitchen help, but I still use my small *molcajete* and *tejolote* (mortar and pestle) for crushing garlic and onion and sometimes chiles. If you are serious about Mexican cooking, you should have one of your own. Why? Because you will find that it pulverizes ingredients more efficiently, producing a savory, more aromatic mix with less effort.

Twenty years ago, as a new bride, I felt lost in trying to cook for my Mexican husband. But with his mother's help—and that of many others, such as Martha, who I watched and helped prepare tamales until I could do it *almost* as well myself, I have slowly learned to cook Mexican food well enough to satisfy the hungriest appetite! Like Paula and Martha, many people will tell you their Mexican cooking secrets. Just ask and don't be afraid to try your own variations. Any recipe can be improved upon and made your very own!

Acknowledgments

Writing this book would have been impossible without the help, support, and encouragement of many people. First, thank you Terry Faulkner, Westport Publishers, Inc., for your decision to go ahead with this project.

Jean and Carolyn Wente, of Wente Bros., Livermore, have been of tremendous help with their encouragement and all of the information about wine in this book. They generously took the time to read the draft typescript and give me specific wine suggestions for individual recipes.

For teaching me how to cook Mexican food, and for providing or helping me with specific recipes, I express my appreciation to Martha Covarrubias, most especially for showing me how to make tamales; to Elena Herrera; and to Sandra Maine, especially for her encouragement.

To my Comadre, Celia Torres, for her generous friendship, help, and advice.

A Paula, mi suegra, con mucho amor le agradesco la guia y asistencia en la hechura de muchas recetas familiares.

To my father, Enoch Haga, thank you for your editorial and word processing skills; and to my mother, Elna, thank you for your help, advice, and proofreading.

Plan of This Book

Because I live on the Wente estate, and have access to many fine wines, I have learned how to combine and enjoy wines with Mexican food. Therefore, I begin this book with a few words on "Mexican Cuisine and Wine," including a section on "Characteristics of Selected Wines," and a short guide to tasting wine.

Then, before the recipe section, I've provided general information and terminology in "Some Mexican Cooking Terms." The recipes in this book are named first in Spanish and then in English. After the recipe section, I conclude with some sample menus.

Please send me your comments and suggestions in care of the publisher. I'll also send you a free list of the brand names that I use in return for a stamped, self-addressed envelope.

Shelia Chávez
Wente Bros. Estate
Livermore, California

Mexican Cuisine and Wine

Probably the most frequent question asked of me is "What wine should I serve with my dinner tonight?" I believe that every cook and every wine aficionado is striving for the perfect match of wine and food. Often beer is considered the only right choice for Mexican cuisine, but wine is an excellent enhancement to many lunch and dinner menus. Wine makes the meal more enjoyable, enhances taste, and brings sophistication to your table. The old guidelines for combining food and wine are being expanded to give you more room for creative expression at your table.

Traditional principles still applicable are: use red wine with meat and white wine with fish; serve white wine before red, and dry wine before sweet. However, these rules, once learned, can be violated. White wine can be served with red meats or dark sauces. Red wines can be served with grilled fish. Experiment to find the combinations most satisfying to you.

Ask yourself whether the flavors of the wine are simple or complex. Wines with outstanding complexity and depth of flavor work well with simple dishes. Simple, straightforward wines are great matches for the more exotic dishes. What is especially important for Mexican cooking is to know that wines with fruit flavors and some residual sugar pair well with hot, spicy dishes.

If food flavors are rich, then a rich wine is needed. Richness enhances richness. If a sauce is creamy, then a buttery, vanillin style Chardonnay will go well with it. Aroma and texture play their part too. If there is an intensity, then the same weight and intensity should be found in the wine. For example, with grilled marinated shrimp dipped in salsa, try a crisp Semillon with a good backbone of fruit flavor.

What you enjoy—what seems right to you—is likely to be enjoyable and right for your family and guests.

Carolyn Wente
Vice President
Wente Bros.
Livermore, California

Characteristics of Selected Wines

To help you plan your meals, some characteristics of a few selected wines are given below. These are Wente Bros. wines, but feel free to use others of your choice. You'll find suggestions for wines to accompany specific dishes throughout this book, all graciously provided by Jean and Carolyn Wente of Wente Bros.

The Wente winery was founded in 1883 by Carl H. Wente; as he introduced cuttings from Europe, the reputation of his wines grew. His sons, Herman and Ernest, made further advances. In 1937 Herman's Sauvignon Blanc won the Grand Prix at the World's Fair and Exposition (in 1889 Wente won America's first Gold Medal for winemaking at the Paris Exhibition).

Ernest's son, Karl, expanded the winery and enhanced its reputation; in 1961 the *Michelin Guide* declared Wente Chardonnay to be the finest white wine in America. Today, Karl's wife Jean and children, Eric, Phillip, and Carolyn, carry on the family tradition of excellence in wine making.

Sauvignon Blanc

Aged in French oak, Sauvignon Blanc is similar in style to the finest dry wines of Bordeaux. A supple, toasty oak flavor complements the rich, floral aroma of the grape.

Semillon

Semillon is a very aromatic grape with a distinctive herbal taste. Goes well with spicy foods, cheese dishes, white meats, and chicken.

Chardonnay

Chardonnay grapes are cold fermented, aged in American oak, and blended to produce the exquisite fragrance, bouquet, and finesse demanded by this temperamental variety. Use with seafood, veal, and pasta with light sauces.

Chardonnay Reserve

Cold fermented, aged in European oak barrels to add depth and complexity. Lush, silky taste with hints of pineapple and citrus. Improves in the bottle with age.

Dry Gewurztraminer

A fragrant wine made in the clean, crisp, dry Alsatian style, Gewurztraminer is especially delicious with light food, salads, or seafood.

Le Blanc de Blancs

The "white of whites" wine has a softer, lighter flavor than other whites. This is a Wente Bros. original blend of Chenin Blanc, White Riesling, and Ugni Blanc grapes. A nice accompaniment to spicy foods.

Johannisberg Riesling

Johannisberg Riesling grapes are grown in the cool, coastal areas of California. A fruity wine, reminiscent of apples and pears, because of its residual sugar. An excellent cocktail wine— or use it with salads, fruits, and cheeses. Good with chiles rellenos or a spicy salsa on fish.

White Zinfandel

White Zinfandel is another cold-fermented wine. Use as a before lunch or dinner cocktail or with a variety of light entrees.

Zinfandel

The Zinfandel grape, well suited to the climate and gravelly soil, has been grown in the Livermore Valley since early in the century. A medium-bodied wine with a zesty, fruity aroma. Here is the perfect match for your roasts and barbecued meats.

Cabernet Sauvignon

Cabernet Sauvignon improves in the bottle with age, growing in subtlety and complexity. A rich, full-flavored wine, ruby

colored, with an intense varietal bouquet. Enjoy this at 55 degrees Fahrenheit, with cheeses, barbecued lamb or beef.

Arroyo Seco Riesling

In exceptional years, Riesling grapes left on the vine past the usual harvest season will be attacked by *Botyritis cinera*, a naturally occurring mold. The result is an exquisite wine with intensified sweetness and unique character. Good with desserts.

Brut Sparkling Wine

Pale gold, very fine bubbles; floral-citrus aroma; fresh peachy fruit flavors. Good with appetizers; a great party wine.

How to Taste Wine

Don't let "wine snobs" fool you! The wine that you like and enjoy is the wine for you. Here are a few tips to help you outdo the sophisticates!

Only your senses can unravel the mysteries of wine. Trust them and you too will become an expert:

Scan: Fill glass with several ounces of wine and grasp by the stem (so your hand doesn't heat the wine). Hold up to the light and evaluate clarity (is it clear or cloudy?) and color.

Sniff: Your first nose-in-the-glass sniff is the most accurate. Check for aroma—an odor particular to the grape and bouquet—a complexity of scents formed only after the wine ages. Do you smell hints of citrus, spice, or fruit?

Swirl: As you swirl the wine, it evaporates more quickly and thus enhances the smell.

Sip: Swish wine around your mouth touching all parts of your tongue—then hold on your palate while breathing in. Note body (the impression wine makes in your mouth) and any tartness, bitterness, or sweetness.

Swallow: Pay attention to the finish (aftertaste), for some flavors appear only now. Write down your impressions and enjoy!

Some Mexican Cooking Terms

Anaheim: see California chiles.

 Ancho: most commonly used chile in México, reddish brown, round, dried and wrinkled; sometimes called pasilla or poblano.

Árbol: dried tree chiles, bright red and very hot.

Blender: in this book, refers to an electric blender, used especially when you have a large quantity of liquid.

Burritos: flour tortillas filled with refried beans, meat, or eggs and salsa.

California chiles: same as Anaheim chiles. Smooth-skinned dried chiles. Mild in flavor and hotness. Dark brown to reddish brown.

Cascabel: dry, small round hot chiles.

Cheeses: imported Mexican cheeses, as well as similar cheese made from goat's milk. Or use Monterey Jack cheese; a variety of this white creamy cheese also comes with chopped chiles having just the desired degree of hotness for certain dishes.

Chicharrones: fried pork skins.

Chiles: many varieties, often with much confusion of names, even in México—see what is available locally and experiment; hotness can be reduced by cleaning out seeds and deveining (though this is rarely done in México).

Chipotle chiles: smoked, dried jalapeños.

Chocolate: Mexicans use a hard, cake-like variety containing chocolate and other spices. This is used in making hot chocolate

and can be used in mole. Montezuma liked his chocolate mixed with honey, flavored with vanilla, and served in a gold cup!

Chorizo: Mexican sausage.

 Cilantro: Chinese parsley, or coriander (the seeds); only the leaves are used.

Cinnamon or Canela: spice from the dried bark of a cinnamon tree. Mexican cinnamon is softer and milder in flavor.

Cumin or Cumino: an aromatic spice in ground powdered form; use sparingly.

Enchiladas: corn tortillas heated (before or after dipping in sauce) and filled with cheese or meat.

Epazote: pungent herb used for flavoring beans, soups, and quesadilla fillings; and to reduce gas caused by eating beans (add one fresh sprig to a pot of beans during the last half-hour of cooking).

 Jalapeños: dark green chile, hot, two or three inches long. Thick skinned. Can be bought fresh or canned.

Lard or Manteca: Mexican shortening. In traditional Mexican cooking, only pork lard is used. Other shortenings or natural, light cooking oils may be substituted. You may like imported olive oil, especially for chicken or fish dishes.

Longaniza: sausage milder than chorizo.

Marjoram: herb, considered a wild oregano, used in seasoning meats and soups.

Masa harina: prepared corn flour available packaged for making tortillas, tamales, and other Mexican dishes.

Masa trigo: instant mix for making flour tortillas.

Molcajete: three-legged stone bowl used with a pestle, or tejolote, for grinding or to purée.

Mole: a delicious sauce made with chiles, spices, nuts, seeds, and chocolate (if desired). Can be served with pork, chicken, turkey, beef, or other meat.

New Mexico chiles: similar to, but hotter, and somewhat more red than the darker brown California chiles.

 Nopales: prickly cactus leaves, usually from *Opuntia tuna*. The fruit is the prickly pear.

Orégano: a favorite herb, available in México in a dozen varieties, often used in Mexican soups and sauces. Imported Mexican oregano is often available locally.

Pasilla chiles: dried, wrinkled, and dark colored; used for making sauces. Also used fresh in cheese or meat stuffing for chiles rellenos. Sometimes confused with the ancho chile because of its shape.

Piquín: a tiny dried round chile, reddish in color and very hot. Used in soups and sauces.

Poblano: sometimes known as ancho or pasilla chiles.

Quesadillas: corn or flour tortillas filled with cheese and grilled to a desired crispness.

Red chili sauce: in this book refers specifically to LAS PALMAS Red Chili Sauce (Salsa de Chili Colorado), made from dry Anaheim chili pods.

Serrano: small, green, very hot chiles. Available fresh or canned.

Tacos: corn tortillas that can be filled with almost anything. Can be served soft, or fried crisp.

Tamales: corn masa and a filling wrapped in corn husks.

Tomatíllos: Mexican green tomatoes used in soups and sauces. Fresh tomatíllos come with a light leafy covering that is removed before rinsing and then cooking. Available canned also, but beware of salt content. Do not substitute American green tomatoes!

Tortas: Mexican sandwich. The torta is made with a soft roll cut in half, then spread with refried beans and then layered with meat, lettuce, and salsa or sliced canned chiles.

Tortillas: México's standard bread. When filling corn tortillas, keep rough side of the tortilla on the inside.

Yellow wax chiles: medium hot yellow chiles two or three inches long. Delicious in sauces, salsa, or as a condiment.

APERITIVOS
Appetizers

Just before completing her cooking, the Mexican housewife typically places some appealing appetizers upon her table; in that way, her family members and guests can begin their meal without delay!

Decorate your table first, if the occasion is special, or just for your own pleasure. Often in México, the women wear beautifully designed aprons while preparing their meals. Whether a formal event, or a family meal, a tablecloth, napkins, simple floral centerpiece, or perhaps just a candle or two, can make the difference between a mundane and a magnificent meal.

Tortilla chips, which are tortillas cut and fried until crisp, served with salsa or a shrimp appetizer, will get your meal off to a good start. Other possibilities are:

- ☐ Refried beans served with freshly made tortilla chips and salsa. Put the beans, chips, and salsa in separate serving dishes.
- ☐ Albóndiguitas, which are simply little meatballs.
- ☐ Guacamole, (avocado dip), served with freshly made tortilla chips. Don't forget the lemon.
- ☐ Shrimp, (aperitivo de camarónes), a favorite of seafood lovers.
- ☐ Small tamales, served with salsa.
- ☐ Small empanadas, (meat pies).

Recommended Wine

Brut, sparkling wine
   (particularly with the camarónes)
Sauvignon Blanc
Le Blanc de Blancs

Aperitivo de Camarónes
Shrimp Appetizer

1/2 pound medium-sized shrimp, cooked

1–3 yellow chiles or serrano, chopped

2 medium-sized tomatoes, peeled and chopped

2–3 tablespoons chopped onions

*juice of 1/2 lemon or lime (or place lemon or lime
    wedges in separate bowls for each serving)*

1–2 tablespoons cilantro (optional)

Clean and rinse shrimp; then place in bowl. Add tomatoes, onions, peppers, and mix with shrimp. Lemon or lime juice can be added at this time, if desired. Salt to taste, or be sure the salt shaker is on the table!

This dish can be varied in several ways. For example, try adding 1 avocado cut into small cubes. By adding lettuce, celery, and avocado, you have a delicious salad.

Serve with tortilla chips. Tortilla chips can be homemade by cutting tortillas and frying them in oil or lard until crisp. Drain on paper towel and then place in bowl near the appetizer.

Serves 4.

Recommended Wines

Brut Champagne
Sauvignon Blanc

Empanaditas
Small Mexican Turnovers

The recipe for these small Mexican turnovers is the same as that for Empanadas, found on page 68. Just make them smaller!—about 3 inches instead of 4 inches in diameter. They are delicious and will disappear as soon as you lay them out.

You can vary this recipe by substituting a package of unbaked crescent rolls for the dough. You may also want to try a self-rising flour, in which case there is no need for the baking powder.

Fill these little gems with whatever your heart desires—not too much cheese, and don't overfill, as they rise while baking.

Suggested Fillings

- A slice of Mexican cheese or Monterey Jack cheese with a slice of Mexican canned chile
- A slice of cooked meat—pork, ham, chicken, or roast beef—with a slice of Mexican canned chile
- Refried beans with a slice of Mexican canned chile
- Leftover cooked roast beef soaked in your favorite salsa, then drained

Recommended Wine

White Zinfandel

Guacamole

Avocado Dip

2 ripe avocados
3 tablespoons onion, minced
2 smashed serrano chiles
1/8–1/4 lemon or lime
dash of salt

Soften the 2 serrano chiles by boiling in water for a few minutes. While the chiles are softening, peel and crush the 2 ripe avocados, but be sure to save the pits, as you will need them later.

Place the crushed avocados in a medium-sized mixing bowl; then add the 3 tablespoons of minced onion. Crush the 2 serrano chiles and add them to the bowl. Squeeze the lemon or lime on top of the mixture and stir well.

Salt lightly, and let your family members or guests add more to suit themselves.

At this time, take a little taste and decide whether or not you'd like to add another serrano chile. If so, boil to soften as before.

Place in a large serving dish with the avocado pits lightly pressed into the top of the mixture. This will help keep the avocado dip from turning brown. (Whenever you use just part of an avocado, always replace the pit to help keep the rest of it fresh and green.)

Guacamole may be served in place of a salsa, or with salsa (use separate serving dishes). Spread on hot corn tortillas for a delicious treat.

Serves 2–4.

Recommended Wine

Sauvignon Blanc

Appetizers

15

Albóndiguitas
Little Meatballs

This recipe is similar to that for Albóndigas (Meat Balls) on page 38.

The Sauce

8 ounces tomato sauce, Mexican style
8 ounces tomato sauce
6-8 cups water

Little Meatballs

1 1/2 pounds lean ground beef
2 small eggs, beaten
1 1/2–2 tablespoons rice, uncooked
1/4 small onion, minced
1/2 teaspoon salt
1/2 teaspoon marjoram powder
1/4 teaspoon garlic powder
1 tablespoon Mexican canned jalapeño peppers, chopped

Combine water and sauces in pot and bring to boil; then reduce heat and simmer for 5 to 10 minutes. Meanwhile, combine all ingredients for meatballs; mix thoroughly.

Bring sauce back to boil. Roll meat into bite-sized balls; drop into boiling sauce. Reduce heat, cover and simmer for 30 minutes. Remove cover, check meatballs. If not ready, cook for an additional 10 to 15 minutes, uncovered.

Drain, then serve hot on decorative toothpicks.

Recommended Wines

Cabernet Sauvignon
Zinfandel

Crema Agria con Jalapeños
Sour Cream Dip with Jalapeños

8 ounces real sour cream
2-6 Mexican canned whole jalapeño peppers
salt to taste

Take jalapeño peppers and mince or crush; then add to sour cream and mix. Begin with two peppers, then add more as needed—these can be hot, so better too few than too many!

Salt to taste.

Place in a serving dish, cover with plastic wrap, and refrigerate for 1 to 2 hours.

Then serve with chips of your choice. Avoid the calories, fat, and sodium of commercially prepared chips. Try making your own from cut up corn tortillas baked at 350–375 degrees until crisp.

Recommended Wine

Johannisberg Riesling

Ensalada de Gallina a la Martha
Martha's Chicken Salad

When served with fried corn tortillas, this favorite recipe can be used as an appetizer.

> *2 potatoes—boiled in jackets, then peeled and*
> *cut into 1 inch cubes*
> *1 chicken—boiled, then diced*
> *5-6 boiled eggs, cut into 1 inch cubes*
> *1-2 Mexican canned jalapeño chiles, diced*
> *6 ounces frozen mixed vegetables— cooked, then drained*
> *1/2 cup liquid from the canned chiles, or 1/2 cup vinegar*
> *1 cup mayonnaise*

Boil chicken parts, in lightly salted water with one large slice of onion and one clove of garlic, until tender. Cool, then dice.

Mix in a large bowl the chicken, potatoes, vegetables, chiles, and chile liquid or vinegar. Add the eggs, then the mayonnaise. Mix well, then salt to taste.

Place salad mixture on top of fried corn tortillas. Shredded lettuce and tomatoes can be added, if desired.

Serves 4 to 6.

Recommended Wine

Sauvignon Blanc

Flautas
Flutes

Here is a delicious party finger food.

1 dozen corn tortillas
1 chicken boiled, chunks or shredded
sour cream
oil or lard
salt to taste

Warm tortillas, one at a time. Place chicken in tortilla, near end, then roll. Secure with toothpick. Fry in oil until crisp. Drain on paper towel. Serve with sour cream, salted to taste, on top.

For an extra touch, shake grated Parmesan cheese, or place minced or diced tomatoes, on top of the sour cream.

Serves 4.

Recommended Wine

Chardonnay Estate Grown

Taquítos
Little Tacos

Small folded or rolled tacos are perfect as a finger food. These can be filled with refried beans or anything else on hand: chicken, meat, cheese.

Soften corn tortillas by heating lightly on a griddle. Fill by placing desired filling in the center. Then fold or roll. Fry to the desired crispness in light cooking oil. Drain on paper towels. Add lettuce or salsa if desired.

Serve immediately.

Tortas
Mexican Sandwich

Tortas can be served as an appetizer or snack. The torta is prepared with a soft roll, somewhat like our French bread, but smaller. If possible, buy your bread for tortas at a Mexican grocery—otherwise, buy soft rolls.

Spread with freshly made refried beans. Layer with either cooked pork, beef, or goat meat. Salsa, or canned sliced chiles and lettuce may be added, if desired.

Recommended Wines

White Zinfandel
Light Cabernet Sauvignon

SopaS

Soups

Soups are a favorite in all nations. They are convenient, easy-to-prepare, and economical. In Mexican cooking, not all soups are liquid as we think of them.

The dry soups are made with rice or pasta and flavored with broth, sauces, and seasonings. They can be served with either sour cream or salsas added to them. Some of the more liquid soups are made by just adding more broth.

Unless the soup itself is the main meal, the soup is served before the main course. Some liquid soups are similar to our stews, so they are a meal in themselves.

Serve soups in large deep bowls; place the family's favorite seasonings on the table so that each person can season to taste just before eating.

Recommended Wines

Chardonnay
Sauvignon Blanc
Zinfandel

Sopas

Sopa a la Mexicana
Soup Mexican Style

8 cups water
1 chicken, cut into parts
3 chicken flavor bouillon cubes
2 carrots, cut into bite size pieces
3 medium potatoes, cut into cubes
1-2 celery ribs, cut into pieces
1 medium tomato, quartered
1 large slice onion
1/4 cup rice, uncooked

Bring 8 cups water to boil in soup pot; add chicken parts. Boil for 5 minutes, skimming off fat and foam. Add 1 large slice onion, cover pot, and simmer for 30 minutes.

Add 1/4 cup uncooked rice, celery, tomato, carrots, and bouillon cubes; bring to boil, cover pot, then simmer for 10 minutes. Add cubed potatoes, cover, and simmer until potatoes are tender.

Serve in soup bowls. Serve with warm tortillas for lunch or dinner. Place salt on table for seasoning to taste, and separate bowls of minced onions, minced green peppers, and lemon or lime wedges.

Serves 4-5.

Recommended Wines

Sauvignon Blanc
Johannisberg Riesling

Sopa de Arroz
Mexican Rice

1 1/3 cups white long-grain rice
1 large slice onion
1 medium clove garlic, crushed
3 small tomatoes (or 3 ounces tomato paste)
2 cups chicken broth or water
1/2 cup cooking oil or lard
dash of salt
2 tablespoons frozen green peas (optional)
1 small carrot, finely diced (optional)

In a bowl rinse rice in cool water twice. Cover rice with cool water and let stand. Place onion, garlic, tomatoes, and 2 cups chicken broth or water in blender and purée (chicken broth or chicken stock can be prepared beforehand for use in this recipe). Add water to bring blender contents to 3 1/2 cups liquid; blend again; and set aside.

Rinse rice again, and drain, and add to oil heated in a large skillet or pan. Cook on medium heat, stirring constantly to prevent rice from burning. Sauté until golden brown. Then drain oil from pan and add tomato mixture from blender. Stir, salt to taste. If desired, add peas and carrots at this time. Bring to boil, cover, and let simmer until liquid is absorbed.

Serves 4–6.

Sopa de Fideo
Vermicelli Soup

Vermicelli or cappellini pasta can be used to make this very popular soup. This recipe is a good change of pace from the rice often served with other Mexican dishes.

6 ounces vermicelli (coiled)
1/2 cup cooking oil or lard
1/2 onion, minced
8 ounces tomatoes, blended
2 cloves garlic, crushed
4–5 cups chicken broth or water
dash of salt

Put vermicelli into small- or medium-sized mixing bowl; using the palms or heels of the hands, break it into small pieces (about 1/4 inch long). Heat oil in deep skillet or 2 quart soup pot. Brown pasta on medium heat; stir to keep from burning and to bring it to a nice even golden brown.

Drain all but one tablespoon of oil from the pan. Then add minced onions to pan and fry lightly for 1 minute. Meanwhile, purée in blender the tomatoes and garlic, and stir into the pan. Add 4-5 cups chicken broth or water and stir again. Cover. The soup is ready when the pasta is tender; otherwise, cook until dry.

For a completely different flavor, add ground cumin seed to the soup while it is cooking. This is pungent, so 2-3 pinches may be enough.

Delicious with sour cream, salsa, and warm tortillas.

Serves 4–6.

Recommended Wine

Johannisberg Riesling (dry, fruity flavor will enhance tomato and chicken base)

Pozole
Pork Stew

This is a stew as well as a soup, so when served as a soup, be sure to serve in deep bowls with plenty of broth. The soup toppings are placed on the table in separate bowls so that each person can season to taste.

Soup

3–4 pounds pork shoulder roast (boneless)
5 pasilla chiles (dry) or 28 ounce can red chili sauce
1 large tomatíllo
1 large slice onion
1 large clove garlic
29 ounce can hominy (white Mexican corn)
salt

Toppings

1 chopped onion
1/2 head cabbage, shredded
3 tablespoons crushed chiles (can be bought prepared)
3 tablespoons dry orégano
1–2 lemons or limes, cut in wedges
1/4 cup cilantro, chopped

Put water on to boil in large soup pot. Trim all fat from pork roast; cut in half; rinse, then add to boiling water. Water should cover the meat. Boil for 5 minutes; skim off foam as it forms. Cover and reduce heat to a simmer where it will be boiling very lightly. Simmer until tender, 1 1/2 to 2 hours.

Meanwhile, remove seeds from pasilla chiles, rinse, and soak in enough boiling water to cover the chiles. Soak for 20 to 30 minutes (save the water). If you prefer the red chili sauce, then all the work has been done for you—just open the can. Put either

your fresh dried chiles (and the water they were soaked in), or the canned sauce, into a blender jar. Be sure the chiles are covered with water. Then add 1 cleaned and rinsed tomatíllo, 1 large clove of garlic, and 1 large slice of onion. Blend on high until all these ingredients are thoroughly ground. Set mixture aside.

When the simmering meat is tender, open the can of hominy and rinse contents in strainer under cool water. Then add hominy to the meat. Now, before adding the chile mixture, skim off the fat from the meat broth (this step is essential to prevent your soup from tasting greasy). Now, remove the meat from the pot, add the chile mixture and bring the soup back to a boil. To keep the meat hot while preventing it from becoming stringy, cut it into 2-inch chunks, cover with foil, and set aside.

Reduce heat to medium; simmer the liquid, uncovered, for 15 minutes. Then, return the meat to the soup pot.

Serve with toppings, salt, and warm tortillas on the table.

Serves 4–6.

Recommended Wine

Sauvignon Blanc (will balance nicely with the rich pork flavor)

Sopa de Cerdo
Pork Soup

3-4 pounds country style pork ribs
1 clove garlic
1 small onion
5 pasilla dry chiles or 20 ounce can red chili sauce
1 tomatíllo
1 small slice of onion
1 teaspoon whole dry Mexican orégano
1/2 cup corn masa (masa harina)
2 tablespoons fresh chopped cilantro
dash of salt

Rinse pork ribs in water; place in soup pot, and cover with water so that the water is at least 1/2 inch above the bones. Bring to boil for 10 minutes. Skim off foam and fat; add the small onion cut into fourths. Then add garlic, cover, and simmer until the meat is tender (about 1 hour).

Meanwhile, clean seeds out of pasilla chiles, rinse, and soak the chiles in hot water for 20 to 30 minutes. Do not pour off the water.

Use part of the water to cover the chiles in the blender jar; add 1 tomatíllo, the small slice of onion, and 1 teaspoon of the whole dry orégano. Blend until smooth.

Add the chile mixture to the tender meat. Stir and bring to boil; cook for 10 minutes.

Then blend together in a large glass 1/2 cup masa and 1 1/2 cups cool water, stirring until well blended. Pour slowly into the soup pot, stirring thoroughly to blend. Add cilantro and cook 10 to 15 minutes. The soup should thicken as it cooks. Salt lightly.

While cilantro is optional for other recipes in this book, in this recipe it is required to enhance the flavor of the masa, broth, and chile.

Serve in soup bowls, along with warm tortillas. Lemon or lime wedges may be served separately to accompany the soup.

Serves 4–6.

Recommended Wine

Zinfandel (good with cilantro, masa and chile flavors)

Sopa de Mostaccioli
Mostaccioli Soup

Here is a recipe worthy of your **molcajete** (mortar). If you don't have one, just crush the garlic and onion on a cutting board.

> *1 1/4 cups dry macaroni—elbow or mostaccioli*
> *1 cup tomatoes, blended*
> *1 small slice onion*
> *1 medium clove of garlic*
> *1/2 cup water*
> *1 tablespoon lard, shortening, or cooking oil*
> *2 cups water*

Bring 8 cups water to a boil; add macaroni; stir. Return to boil, cook on medium high until tender. Drain, rinse in cool water, and then place in cool water until ready to use.

Crush garlic and onion in your **molcajete**, until smooth; then add 1/2 cup water and mix with the **tejolote** (pestle). Melt 1 tablespoon of lard in a medium-sized pot; then add the garlic, onion, and water mixture from the **molcajete**. Stir and cook for 1 minute at a low boil. Add the blended tomatoes, and 2 cups of water, and bring back to a boil at medium heat. Boil lightly for 5 minutes; then add the drained macaroni. Bring back to low boil at medium heat for 3 to 5 minutes. Salt lightly.

If larger macaroni is desired, do not serve immediately, but set aside so that the macaroni will have time to absorb some of the liquid. Serve as a soup or as a meal for lunch or dinner. Great with sour cream, freshly made tomato salsa, and tortillas.

Serves 4–6.

Recommended Wine

Sauvignon Blanc

CARNES Y BARBACOAS

Meats and Barbecues

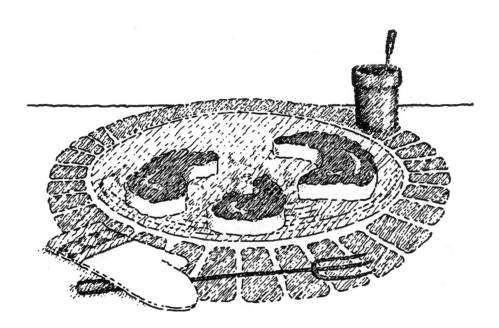

In México, meats are neither cut nor prepared as they are in the United States. While turkey, chicken, pork, beef, and goat are all popular, lamb and fish are eaten less often. Mexican women like to stretch their food budgets by using meats in soups and sauces so that they will go a long way. And, while many Mexicans may use beans, potatoes, and other vegetables in preparing tacos and enchiladas, my mother–in–law Paula uses meat.

Today, many people, Mexicans and gringos alike, cook over outdoor charcoal grills. A typical Mexican barbecue makes use of a huge, deep, copper bowl, or **caso**, which is set into a pit dug in the ground. After the pit is dug, a fire is lit and allowed to burn down, at which time the **caso** is placed over the hot ashes.

Cooking a whole pig, for example, takes much time, and the cook is usually at the fire the whole time. This gives the men, chilled beer or tequila in hand, an excuse to gather 'round, laughing, socializing, and telling their latest tales, whether tall or short! The women gather in small groups of their own, where they chat, gossip, and drink tequila, beer, wine, or soft drinks as they prepare the food that accompanies the barbecue.

After a good meal has been enjoyed by all, the day is usually at an end with darkness falling. Then the music of the guitars becomes more intense—the evening finally concluding with singing and dancing.

Here are some typical menus for barbecues:

Barbecue Pig

Barbecue Pig
Boiled Chicken
Mole
Rice
Beans
Mexican Canned Chiles or Salsa
Tortillas

Barbecue Chicken and Beef

Barbecue Chicken and Beef
Marcaroni Salad
Guacamole
Beans
Corn on the Cob
Salsa
Tortillas
Lemon Cake

and, of course,
wine, beer, or other beverages of your choice

Recommended Wines

Cabernet Sauvignon (enhances and picks up the
   rich flavors in mole sauce)
Chardonnay Reserve

Carne Asada
Grilled Meat

3–4 pounds rump roast (sliced very thin),
   or eye of round roast
seasoned meat tenderizer

Grill outside, or to prepare inside, cover griddle with aluminum foil, then preheat on medium heat. Take one slice of beef at a time, season, pierce meat with fork, sprinkle on tenderizer, and place on griddle. To prevent saltiness, you may wish to tenderize just one side of the meat. Continue until the griddle is covered with sliced meat.

Turn meat over when brown. The meat will cook in its own juices, adding to its tenderness. Place each cooked slice in foil to keep it warm; replace it immediately on the griddle with another uncooked slice until all the meat is cooked.

Serve in warm corn or flour tortillas with your favorite salsa, or with rice, refried beans, salsa, and freshly warmed tortillas. Also delicious with macaroni or potato salad, fresh salsa and warmed tortillas. Good for lunch or dinner.

Recommended Wine

Cabernet Sauvignon

Carne Asada en Olla a la Abuela
Grandmother's Pot Roast

This recipe, one of my grandmother's, is simple, easy, and versatile. I have used it for many years. The cooked meat is a delight because it can be cooked and served in so many different ways. After the meat is cooked, either serve it with potatoes and carrots cooked in the juice of the pot roast, or with gravy made from the juice of the roast; or flavor it with your favorite red or green salsa or chile sauce by adding it to the sauce and cooking for an additional minute or so. Use it as a soft taco by placing the cut or shredded meat on warm corn tortillas, with beans or salsa if desired. Use as a burrito by placing refried beans on warm flour tortillas, adding the shredded meat cooked in salsa or sauce, and then rolling the tortillas. Many times I have made a lunch of these burritos for my husband, Arturo, when he couldn't come home for a meal. They can be kept warm by wrapping in foil and placing in a warmed thermos.

seasoned meat tenderizer
3–4 pounds rump roast, sirloin roast, cross rib roast,
*   eye of round roast, or even a large sirloin steak*
1/2 cup water
2 tablespoons lard, shortening, or cooking oil

Pierce meat with fork; sprinkle on tenderizer. Heat and melt 2 tablespoons lard in large stew pot. Then add roast and brown on all sides. Add 1/2 cup water, bring to boil, cover and simmer on low heat until tender, 2 to 3 hours.

Serves 4–6.

Recommended Wine

Zinfandel

Meats and Barbecues

Bistec a la Mexicana
Beefsteak Mexican Style

2–3 pounds sirloin steak, filet mignon, or round steak
   (ask butcher to tenderize round steak)
seasoned meat tenderizer
8-ounce can tomato sauce, Mexican style,
   or 8–ounces homemade light salsa

Heat oven to 350 degrees. Place steak in baking dish and sprinkle with tenderizer. Pierce all over with fork, then place in oven for 20 minutes.

Remove from oven, pour sauce over steak, and return to oven for 10 to 20 minutes, depending upon how well done you like your steak.

Serve with rice, refried beans, and warm tortillas for lunch or dinner.

Serves 4–6.

Recommended Wine

Cabernet Sauvignon

Carne con Papas y Zanahorias
Meat with Potatoes and Carrots

2 pounds sirloin steak or small beef roast

2 tablespoons cooking oil or lard

seasoned meat tenderizer

1/2 cup water

3 potatoes, cut into chunks

3 carrots, cut into chunks

2 sliced fresh chiles (optional)

Use fork to pierce meat, sprinkle on tenderizer, turn meat over, and repeat. Heat oil in stew pot, add meat, and brown on all sides. Add 1/2 cup water, bring to boil, cover, and lower heat to simmer until tender.

Remove meat and place in covered dish. Add carrots and potatoes to stew pot; add water if needed; cook until tender.

Slice the meat and serve with the potatoes and carrots and warm tortillas.

Serves 4–6.

Recommended Wine

Cabernet Sauvignon

Albóndigas
Meat Balls

For variety, here are two alternative recipes. Either of them can be served with rice or beans, warm tortillas, and freshly made salsa.

> 1 pound lean ground beef
> 2 eggs, beaten
> 1 1/2 tablespoons rice, uncooked
> 1/4 small onion, minced
> 1/2 teaspoon salt
> 1/2 teaspoon marjoram powder
> 1/4 teaspoon garlic powder

or

> 1 pound lean ground beef
> 1 potato, minced
> 1 1/2 tablespoons rice, uncooked
> 1/4 small onion, minced
> 1/2 teaspoon salt
> 1/4 teaspoon poultry seasoning
> 2 eggs, beaten

Sauce

> 8 ounces tomato sauce, Mexican style, or your own salsa

and

> 8 ounces tomato sauce
> 6–8 cups water

or

> 16 ounces tomato sauce
> 6-8 cups water

Combine water and sauces (or sauce and salsa) in pot and bring to boil, then reduce heat and simmer for 5 to 10 minutes. Meanwhile, combine all ingredients for meatballs; mix thoroughly.

Bring sauce back to a boil. Roll meat into balls, rounded tablespoon size, and drop into hot boiling sauce. Reduce heat, cover, and simmer for 40 minutes. Remove cover, check meatballs. If not ready, cook for additional 15 to 20 minutes uncovered.

Serve with rice or beans, fresh salsa, and warm tortillas. Serves 4–6.

Recommended Wines

Cabernet Sauvignon
Zinfandel

Chile Colorado al Arturo
Arturo's Meat in Red Chile Sauce

Cook this delicious dish for serving tomorrow when it will taste even better! Can be served not only with rice and refried beans, but also with refried beans as a filler for burritos.

Before cooking, try tenderizing the meat with a prepared meat tenderizer.

The ground cumin seed is an **essential** ingredient. It adds flavor and removes the bite from the dry chiles.

2–2 1/2 pounds lean sirloin steak, cut into cubes
7 dry California chiles, remove stems
1 dry pasilla chile, remove stems
2–3 tablespoons oil or lard
2 cloves garlic, crushed with 1 teaspoon water
1 cup canned tomatoes, blended
1/2 cup tomato sauce, Mexican style, or homemade salsa
2 pinches ground orégano
2-3 pinches ground cumin seed
2 tablespoons flour
1/2 cup water
salt

Heat oil in stew pot; then add cubed meat. Stir, then cover. Turn heat to medium, and stir from time to time to cook evenly until tender.

Meanwhile, rinse the dry chiles, place in sauce pan, and cover with water. Bring to boil, cover, then simmer for 10 to 15 minutes.

When the meat is tender, drain oil, add crushed garlic, stir, and cook for 1 minute.

Place the chiles and water in the blender, 3 to 3 1/2 cups total mixture; blend and strain mixture to remove seeds and lumps. Add to the cooked meat. Stir, and turn heat to medium.

Mix flour with 1/2 cup water, stirring until smooth. Then pour through strainer into the stew pot. Stir well. Then add the tomatoes, tomato sauce (Mexican style), and seasonings. Stir. Bring to boil, then simmer on medium heat for 5 to 10 minutes, uncovered.

This is a favorite for lunch or dinner when served with rice, refried beans, salsa, and flour or corn tortillas.

Recommended Wines

 Cabernet Sauvignon
White Zinfandel

Chile Colorado
Meat in Red Chile Sauce

This recipe can be made in a seemingly infinite number of ways, all delicious. For example, I've seen it made with dried chile pods, dried chile powder, and also with fresh tomatoes and fresh green chiles. But, it is always served with Mexican rice and refried beans, fresh salsa, and freshly made tortillas.

4 pounds sirloin steak, or filet mignon,
*   cut into 1-inch cubes*
1/3 cup tomato sauce
8-ounce can red chili sauce
1/4 teaspoon garlic powder
1/4 teaspoon chile powder
pinch of ground cloves
1/8 teaspoon ground cumin seed
2 rounded tablespoons cooking oil or lard
5-7 rounded tablespoons flour
salt

In a large pot, place the meat and cover with cool water. Bring to boil, and boil for 3 to 5 minutes, skimming off fat and foam as needed. Add the remaining ingredients except for the flour and lard. Bring to boil. Reduce heat, cover, and simmer until meat is tender, 1 to 1 1/2 hours.

Then add the lard to a skillet, heat, and brown the flour, stirring as needed. Gradually add this browned flour to the meat and sauce. Stir continuously so that the flour will mix well with the sauce. Cook 7 to 10 minutes, uncovered, stirring as needed to prevent the sauce from burning, until the sauce reaches the desired thickness.

Salt to taste, or place salt on the table. Serve with rice and beans or as a filling for burritos.

Serves 5–8.

Recommended Wine

Cabernet Sauvignon

Chiles y Cebollas con Carne

Peppers and Onions with Meat

2 pounds sirloin steak
2-4 tablespoons cooking oil or lard
1 small to medium onion
2 or more yellow or green chile peppers
salt

Cut the meat into medium-sized strips. Heat lard in skillet on medium heat. Brown the meat, cover and sauté; stir from time to time, so that the meat cooks evenly. After 5 minutes, reduce heat to low and continue cooking, covered; stir occasionally.

Meanwhile, clean and rinse the chiles and onions and cut them into strips. When the meat is tender, add the strips to the meat in the skillet. Stir, cover, and simmer until tender.

Salt to taste or place salt on the table. Can be served as a taco or burrito filler; also can be served with rice or beans or dry vermicelli soup.

Serves 4–6.

Recommended Wine

 Zinfandel

Lasagne a la Mexicana
Mexican Lasagne

This is my father's accidental invention! My father likes it cold the day after preparation, but it can be served hot or cold.

> 6–9 flour tortillas (thick, 8-inch diameter)
> 1 1/2 pounds chicken, pork, or beef, baked or boiled and shredded
> refried beans
> salsa
> 6-8 ounces cheddar cheese, shredded

Place 2 or 3 flour tortillas in bottom of 8 inch pie pan or square baking dish. Spread thickly with refried beans; then a layer of shredded meat. Top with salsa, then shredded cheese. Repeat until you have 2 or 3 layers. Bake at 350 degrees until hot or cheese is melted; about 10 minutes.

Top with a decorative layer of sour cream and guacamole, sprinkled with a few pitted and sliced black olives. Other toppings, such as salsa, onions, and lettuce may be added.

Serves 6–8.

Recommended Wines

Semillon (with pork)
Zinfandel (with beef and pork)
Chardonnay (with chicken)

Albondigón a la Lety
Lety's Meatloaf

1 1/2 pounds lean ground beef

15 soda crackers, crushed

8 ounces tomato sauce

1 clove garlic, minced

1 large slice of onion, minced

1 egg, beaten

1 small carrot, finely chopped

1 small potato, peeled and finely chopped

Combine all ingredients in large mixing bowl. Mix and set aside. Place foil in bottom of 8 1/2-inch by 12 1/2-inch glass dish, leaving enough foil to wrap up over the meatloaf. Place meatloaf, round shaped, on foil in glass dish; fold foil up over the meatloaf, but leave enough room inside the foil for the fat to cook away from the meat.

Seal the foil and place dish in 375-degree oven for 1 1/4 hours; as soon as carrots and potatoes are tender the meatloaf is ready to serve with cooked vegetables, salsa, and warm tortillas; or, serve with cooked vegetables, baked potatoes, or little potato cakes (see recipe page 97).

Serves 4.

Recommended Wine

Cabernet Sauvignon

Guisado Mexicano
Mexican Stew

When I first started cooking this recipe, I used cooked canned pork with tomato sauce, Mexican hot style, and found it to be quite tasty. Since the canned meat is already cooked, it only needs to be fried lightly until brown. But remember, if you do not use sirloin, a 12–ounce can of cooked pork won't require 3 to 4 tablespoons of oil!

> 1 pound sirloin steak or 12–ounce can cooked pork
> 4 medium potatoes
> 16 ounce can cut green beans
> 1/2 small onion
> 3-4 tablespoons cooking oil or lard
> 3–4 cups water
> 8-ounce can tomato sauce, Mexican style,
>   or red chili sauce
> salt

Cut sirloin into 3/4 to 1 inch cubes. Heat oil in a medium-sized soup pot. Brown sirloin on medium low heat, covered. Keep checking meat and stirring occasionally. If meat is not tender by the time the bottom of the pot is dry, then add 2 ounces water and simmer on low, covered, until tender.

Meanwhile, mince onion or cut into ringlets. Set onions aside. Cut potatoes into 3/4 to 1 inch cubes and place in bowl; cover potatoes with water to keep them from turning brown. Set potatoes aside.

When meat is tender, add onions and sauté for 2 minutes. Drain water from potatoes and add them to the pot with the meat and onions. Sauté for 1 to 2 minutes. Then add a can of your preferred sauce, and 3 to 4 cups of water, depending upon how hot or flavored with tomato you like it. Bring to boil. Add the green beans. Bring back to medium boil, cover, and simmer until

potatoes are tender. By covering the pot, the potatoes will cook faster.

Remember, the potatoes are in hot liquid, so they should be served immediately—or else cut their cooking time so that they won't be mushy.

Salt to taste, or place salt on table.

Can be served with rice or beans on the side, or just as a soup. Serve with fresh warm tortillas and Mexican canned chiles.

Serves 4.

Recommended Wine

Cabernet Sauvignon

Mostrador para Tacos a la Madre
Mother's Taco Buffet

This taco buffet was introduced by my mother especially for outdoor family gatherings (where it quickly disappears).

1 pound kidney beans

2 pounds lean ground beef

2-3 tablespoons seasoned chile powder

8-ounce can tomato sauce

1 package of taco mix

1 cup cornmeal or cornbread mix

1 large bag tortilla chips

1 head of lettuce, chopped

1–2 onions, chopped

3-4 tomatoes, chopped

1/2-1 pound mild cheddar cheese, grated

avocado dip or guacamole

1/2 pint sour cream

Mexican canned jalapeño or serrano chiles (optional)

1 can pitted and sliced black olives

Cook kidney beans in water until tender. (Do not add salt because this hardens the skins.) Brown 2 pounds of lean ground beef, drain fat. Add chile powder, taco mix, and tomato sauce; stir. Add 1 cup liquid from the beans, stir again, and bring to a boil. Lower heat, and cook for 4 to 5 minutes. Add mixture to the beans, stir, bring to boil, and cook 5 minutes. Add cool water to cornmeal or cornbread mix and stir to dissolve thoroughly. Add to beans through a strainer. Mix and cook 10 to 15 minutes; stir often to prevent burning.

Arrange the dishes on the buffet in order so that those in line will first place tortilla chips on plate, then add the beans and meat, then cheese and lettuce, then onions and tomatoes, and finally sour cream and avocado dip, and chiles and olives. Or serve the ingredients at the table in separate bowls or serving dishes.

Serves 4–6. Double or triple the recipe for larger gatherings.

Recommended Wine

White Zinfandel

Milanesa
Breaded Steak

2-3 pounds sirloin steak, thick cut
2-3 packages from a box of soda crackers (crushed
  with a rolling pin)
2 eggs
cooking oil or lard, as needed
seasoned meat tenderizer
garlic powder

Slice sirloin steak lengthwise very thin, either 2 x 4 inches, or 4 x 4 inches. On one side of the sliced meat, shake sparingly small amounts of tenderizer. Then pierce or poke it in with a fork. Then, on the other side of the meat, shake garlic powder sparingly.

Heat enough oil in a frying pan to cover the bottom of the pan (a Teflon pan is preferable). Meanwhile, beat the eggs. Dip sliced steak in the eggs and then into the crackers. Sauté until tender and brown on both sides. As each slice is finished, drain and place in foil to keep it warm.

Serve for lunch or dinner along with rice or beans and fresh salsa and warm tortillas. Also delicious with avocado salad and warm tortillas.

Serves 6.

Recommended Wine

Cabernet Sauvignon

Lomo de Cerdo en Chile Verde
Loin of Pork in Green Chile Sauce

Here is a popular and delicious pork dish.

1 pound lean pork (or beef) cut into 1-inch cubes

1 large clove garlic

1/4 cup water

1/2 pound tomatíllos, cleaned, rinsed, and boiled in water
    (save the water)

2-5 chiles, red, green, or dried (árbol dry chiles)

salt

1 tablespoon chopped cilantro (optional)

Brown pork until tender in 2 to 4 tablespoons of oil, medium heat. Then crush 1 clove garlic in **molcajete**, adding 1/4 cup water to garlic. Mix, then add to tender pork. Simmer for 1 to 2 minutes; then add blended cooked tomatíllos, chiles, and the 1/2 to 3/4 cup water in which the tomatíllos were boiled. Stir and cook for 5 to 10 minutes to the desired thickness.

Salt to taste or place salt on table. Serve with rice, beans, and warm tortillas for lunch or dinner. For breakfast, serve over fried eggs with fresh refried beans and warm tortillas.

Recommended Wines

Johannisberg Riesling
Le Blanc de Blancs

Tomates y Tomatíllos con Carne de Puerco

Pork with Tomatoes

This dish, one of my husband's favorites, is my own version of pork with tomatoes. This recipe can be made with or without tomatíllos. For a rich savory dish add fresh red tomatoes, beefsteak variety, or Roma tomatoes with tomatíllos.

> 1 1/2 pounds pork chops, boneless sirloin cut
>   (1/4 inch by 1 inch strips)
> 2 cloves garlic, crushed with 3 tablespoons water
> 6 tomatoes, equal to 1 1/2–2 cups blended tomatoes
> 6 tomatíllos, boiled in advance
> 6 serrano chiles
> 2-3 tablespoons light cooking oil or lard

Heat oil in deep pan; brown pork lightly for 2 minutes on low heat, stirring often. Cover and simmer on low heat, stirring from time to time. When tender, add garlic and water. Stir. Cook for 1 to 2 minutes.

Blend tomatoes, tomatíllos, and chiles. Add mixture to pork; stir. Bring to boil, cover and simmer on low heat for 10 to 15 minutes. Salt to taste. Serve with rice, or beans, or over eggs, or as a filler for burritos.

Serves 2–3.

Recommended Wine

Chardonnay Reserve

Carnitas
Tender Pork Bits

Carnitas are small cuts of pork cooked until very tender. Mexicans cook this dish best in their famous outdoor pots, **casos**. The meat can be cooked indoors, but the flavor is much different. Many times I have watched my *comadre* (my son's godmother) make carnitas in her kitchen; she adds a red sauce she prepares with dry chiles and seasonings as a filler for tamales.

In this recipe, you may cut lean pork into cubes or strips which fit easily into warmed tortillas. A recipe variation is possible by adding 1 to 3 sliced fresh serrano chiles to the meat just as it is almost done; then cook the chiles with the meat until tender.

> *2-3 pounds lean pork*
> *3-4 tablespoons cooking oil or lard*
> *1/4 cup water, if needed*
> *1–3 fresh serrano chiles, sliced (optional)*
> *salt*

Cut lean pork into 1 to 2 inch strips or into 1 inch cubes. Heat skillet, on medium heat, to melt lard. Add pork; fry until brown, stirring as needed. Turn heat to low, cover skillet, and cook until tender. If needed, add 1/4 cup water to keep meat from burning. Salt to taste or place salt on table. Serve in warm tortillas with salsa. Rice can be added to make an even better taco.

Serves 4–6.

Recommended Wine

Sauvignon Blanc

Arroz con Pollo
Rice with Chicken

This simple dish is a favorite of my children. Using the same recipe as that for Mexican Rice (see **Sopa de Arroz** on page 24), but before browning the rice, rinse and cut a small frying chicken into serving pieces. Brown the chicken pieces on all sides in 1/2 cup light cooking oil or melted lard. Remove chicken from pan, and set pieces aside to drain off oil or lard.

Take your rinsed rice and brown in the same oil until golden brown. Drain oil from pan, and add tomato mixture to rice. Bring to boil and place chicken in the boiling liquid. If desired, carrots and frozen peas can now be added. The carrots must be thinly sliced, either across or lengthwise, so that they will cook evenly with the chicken and rice. Cover and simmer until the liquid is absorbed.

Serve with potato salad, salsa, and warm tortillas for lunch or dinner.

Serves 4–6.

Recommended Wines

Chardonnay
Semillon
Zinfandel

Pollo a la Mexicana
Mexican Chicken

1 chicken, whole or cut

8-ounce can tomato sauce

8-ounce can tomato sauce, Mexican style

16-24 ounces water

2 medium potatoes, peeled and quartered

2 medium carrots, peeled and sliced

1 medium zucchini squash, sliced

Cut chicken into pieces; place in large skillet, but add no oil. Add potatoes, carrots and zucchini with tomato sauce, and enough water to cover all vegetables and chicken. Bring to a boil, cover, and simmer for 1 hour or until the chicken is tender.

Serve for lunch or dinner with warm tortillas, fresh salsa, or a can of Mexican chiles.

Serves 4.

Recommended Wines

Chardonnay
Zinfandel

Pollo Relleno a la Mexicana
Mexican Stuffed Chicken

1 whole fryer, ready to stuff

Stuffing:

1/2–3/4 pounds lean ground chuck
(depending on size of chicken)
2 tablespoons carrots, finely chopped
1 teaspoon onion, finely chopped
2 tablespoons potatoes, finely chopped
1 small clove of garlic, crushed
2 tablespoons frozen peas
salt

Mix stuffing ingredients together with the exception of the frozen peas. Brown stuffing mix in a skillet to remove any redness from the meat. Add peas. Drain fat, and stuff chicken with the mixture. Butter top of the chicken lightly, then salt.

Place stuffed chicken in foil and wrap, first one way; then the other way with another piece of foil. Place chicken in glass dish. Bake at 400 degrees for 1 hour. Then bake for an additional 1 1/2 to 2 hours at 350 degrees. Test chicken for doneness by poking top of breast with a fork. Serve for dinner with sliced cooked potatoes, carrots, salsa, and warm tortillas.

Serves 4–5.

Recommended Wines

Sauvignon Blanc
Semillon

Carnes y Barbacoas

Huevos
Eggs

As I learned by visiting my husband's native country, there is no limit to the Mexican imagination when it comes to cooking eggs. Omelets can be made by adding different meats, such as chorizo or chicken, as fillers. Tomatoes, chiles, or onions can be added for still further variation, or used alone.

The omelet is so versatile and satisfying that it can be served for breakfast, lunch, or dinner. And don't be afraid to experiment—it's hard to do anything wrong!

Chorizo con Huevos
Chorizo with Eggs

This recipe can be made in any number of ways by adding a few teaspoons of minced onions, peppers, or tomatoes, as desired. Try it with refried beans for still another variation.

4 ounces chorizo
2 or 3 eggs
1–2 tablespoons milk (optional)
salt to taste

Remove skin from the chorizo and mash with fork in skillet while frying over medium heat. Fry until tender, about 5 minutes. Beat eggs together, adding milk if desired; then add egg mixture to chorizo in skillet. Stir until eggs are cooked.

Serve with refried beans, tortillas, and salsa. Can be served for breakfast, lunch, or dinner. Double the recipe for a cozy Sunday twosome!

Recommended Wines

Gewurztraminer
Sauvignon Blanc

Eggs

Tortilla a la Mexicana
Mexican Omelet

2 eggs
1 chile pepper, finely chopped
1 teaspoon finely chopped onion
1 or more tablespoons cooked chicken meat, shredded
1 tablespoon milk
cooking oil or lard, as needed

Beat 2 eggs with milk, chopped pepper, and chopped onion combined. Heat cooking oil or lard on medium heat in fry pan, then add egg mixture. Cook as you would a plain omelet, but before turning sides in, add shredded chicken. Then turn and continue cooking until egg mixture is firm.

If desired, place one or two slices of cheese over the omelet when served.

Serves 1.

Huevos al Arturo
Arturo's Eggs

2-3 eggs
3-4 tablespoons tomato or tomatíllo salsa, warmed
oil
salt

Take small skillet and heat oil on low. Fry eggs lightly on both sides. Turn out onto plate. Pour or spoon out the desired amount of fresh, warm tomato or tomatíllo salsa.

Serve with refried beans, sliced and fried canned meat, and freshly warmed corn or flour tortillas.

Serves 1.

Recommended Wines

Gerwurztraminer
Sauvignon Blanc

Huevos

Huevos con Tortillas
Eggs with Tortillas

Use yesterday's tortillas for today's breakfast Here's the secret:

1 corn tortilla, cut into bite sized pieces
2 tablespoons light cooking oil
2 or 3 eggs, beaten
2–3 tablespoons milk, if desired
2 tablespoons cooked ham steak, sliced or diced

Fry the cut tortilla lightly in oil. Add ham and fry lightly. Combine eggs and milk, beat, and pour over the ham and tortillas. Scramble to suit.

Serve with fresh salsa and tortillas.

Serves 1–2.

Recommended Wines

Gewurztraminer
Sauvignon Blanc

Huevos Revueltos a la Mexicana
Mexican Scrambled Eggs

Here is a quick breakfast for a busy morning easily prepared with a minimum of hustle and bustle.

> *3 eggs*
> *1 tablespoon butter or light cooking oil*
> *1 tablespoon milk*
> *8-ounce can tomato sauce, Mexican style*
>   *or*
> *8 ounces tomato salsa*
>   *or*
> *2 or 3 fresh tomatoes*
> *1 teaspoon onion, finely chopped*
> *1 small chile pepper, finely chopped*

If using tomato salsa or tomato sauce, beat eggs and milk together, then scramble in butter. Add salsa or tomato sauce. Stir and simmer for 2 to 3 minutes, then serve.

If using fresh tomatoes, peel and cut finely. Then beat eggs, milk, tomatoes, onions, and chile pepper together. Scramble in butter.

Serves 1–2.

Recommended Wine

Brut champagne

MAIZ Y TRIGO
Corn and Wheat

The **tortilla** is the Mexican bread! Many years ago, due to the lack of machinery, much of the corn for household use was ground by hand. Arturo, my husband, as a small boy, sold the corn tortillas that his mother, Paula, made day in and day out. Now, of course, Paula sends one of her children to a nearby store to buy them ready made; the custom is to send the child with a cloth to wrap the tortillas in; these are then placed in a basket until the meal is served.

Masa, a wheat, white, or corn flour, is to Mexicans what grain is to other Americans. Corn tortillas, tamales, and many other dishes are made from masa. Mexicans also eat a bread somewhat like our French bread; these are made up as individual rolls to be eaten at meals as is, or as **tortas**, a kind of sandwich.

Sweet breads, somewhat like our sweet rolls or coffee cakes, are also eaten for breakfast with chocolate or coffee.

Blue corn flour may be used for preparing blue colored corn chips, tortillas, tostadas, tacos, and enchiladas. Blue corn grows both in the United States and in México. Most of this is used for commercial products, such as chips, but you can adapt the idea for your own party treats.

Today, in many parts of the United States, you can buy masa already prepared for you. If not available in your area, corn and wheat masa is often available packaged in ready mix (just add water).

Enchiladas

Enchiladas are **corn** tortillas flavored by dipping in sauce before or after frying lightly, then filled with meat or cheese and rolled.

All of the fillings can be prepared ahead of time. The sauce can be precooked. The cheese and meat can be shredded in advance, after the meat is cooked.

This is the Mexican quick lunch! Enchiladas cook up fast and they are best when served and eaten as soon as they are ready. They can be reheated in the microwave at low power, or they can be kept warm at 325 degrees for no more than 10 minutes. But first, put some (not too much, or they will get soggy) enchilada sauce on top to keep them from drying out.

Tacos

Tacos are warmed **corn** tortillas, filled with whatever you like, folded or rolled, and then fried (if desired). They are typically served with garnishes. While in México I saw tacos being served in two ways:

1. Warm the tortillas, fill with cooked chicken, beef, steak, pork, goat meat, or refried beans. Roll and fry lightly to the desired crispness. Serve with sour cream and salsa or with other vegetables.

2. Warm the tortilla, fill with meat, freshly cooked beans, and salsa.

Tortillas

For a number of years I made my own corn and flour tortillas until I found a Mexican café that sells them freshly made and just as good as my own. Buy thicker flour tortillas as these won't fall apart on you before you are finished warming or filling them!

If you prefer to do it yourself, you may purchase fine masa harina or masa trigo to which you just add water and mix. When I make flour tortillas I use the masa trigo with warm water; follow directions on the package, except let the masa raise for 30 minutes instead of 20 because then the masa is easier to roll out.

If you prefer to make your tortillas from scratch (go ahead—try it at least once!), this is an excellent recipe:

> *2 cups enriched all-purpose flour, presifted*
> *1/2 teaspoon baking powder*
> *1 teaspoon salt*
> *2 tablespoon shortening or lard*
> *1/2–1 cup warm water*

Sift flour, salt, and baking powder into mixing bowl. Then add lard and mix with fingers and hands. Add water and mix into a stiff (but not sticky) dough. Knead 3 to 5 minutes. Divide into 6 to 12 balls, depending upon the size tortilla you prefer. Cover 20 to 30 minutes with a kitchen towel.

Then roll out each ball separately on a lightly floured board. Preheat an ungreased griddle, then cook the tortillas on medium heat until lightly browned; turn only once. Place on thin towel, and when cool wrap in towel and cover with foil or place in plastic bag.

If you are preparing burritos for someone to take for lunch, wrap the filled tortillas in foil and place them in a warm thermos. Otherwise they may fall apart should they absorb any moisture.

Burritos

Burritos are simply **flour** tortillas filled with almost anything from meatloaf, chile colorado, or refried beans to eggs. There are no fancy ways to make burritos. They are simply flour tortillas, preferably thick, warmed, filled, and wrapped (rolled).

If away from home, wrap burritos in foil and place in a warmed thermos. Can be served for lunch or dinner.

Recommended Wines

Red Zinfandel (with beans and beef)
Sauvignon Blanc (with chicken)

Empanadas
Empanadas

Empanadas are a Mexican filled pastry served for dessert, snacks, or with meals.

1 cup all-purpose flour, presifted
1 teaspoon baking powder
1/2 teaspoon salt
1/4 cup lard or shortening
3 tablespoons ice water
filling of your choice

Into a mixing bowl, sift together the flour, baking powder, and salt. Add lard; with pastry blender or fingers, blend together with flour. Then add just enough ice water for the dough to hold together.

Divide dough into 6 pieces. Roll out each piece on a floured board to make a round shape about 4 inches in diameter. Put in a spoonful of your favorite filling (see below), fold over, and seal edges. Deep fry in hot oil or bake at 375-400 degrees for 10-15 minutes or until light golden brown.

Makes 6 empanadas.

Suggested fillings

To make empanadas that are more like our dessert pastries, fill with sugar and cinnamon, jam, or fruit preserves.

For a savory empanada, fill with cooked meat in sauce or with cooked chicken in chile and cheese. For lunch, try filling with refried beans with sliced canned chile and grated cheese—or with ham and cheese with sliced canned chile.

Recommended Wines

Brut Champagne
Late Harvest Riesling

Quesadillas
Tortillas with Cheese

12 corn or flour tortillas
1/2–1 pound Mexican cheese
    or
Monterey Jack cheese (sliced thin)
    or
Monterey Jack cheese with chiles

Gently heat the tortillas to soften them; add the cheese, fold in half, and heat on ungreased griddle at medium heat until the cheese is melted. Turn often to keep from burning. Can be cooked to any desired degree of crispness.

Serve as a snack or serve with refried beans and salsa or Mexican canned chiles for lunch or dinner.

Makes 12 quesadillas.

Recommended Wine

 Johannisberg Riesling

Corn and Wheat

Tacos de Papas
Potato Tacos

These delicious potato tacos are a great lunch or party treat.

4–5 potatoes
cooking oil or lard, as needed
1/2 head lettuce
sour cream
homemade salsa
12 corn tortillas

Boil 4 to 5 potatoes until tender (easy to put a fork through), cool, peel, and mash. Salt to taste.

Take corn tortillas and warm one at a time; on half of each tortilla, place 2 or 3 tablespoons of mashed potatoes; then fold over to make a half-moon shape. Do this as you go along, and do them ahead of time and wrap in foil.

Heat approximately 1/2 cup light cooking oil or lard in frying pan (you will need more oil or lard as you go along) and fry 2 or 3 tacos at a time (depending upon the size of your frying pan). Fry until tacos reach the desired crispness. Drain on paper towels. Garnish with lettuce, sour cream, and salsa.

Makes 12 tacos.

Recommended Wine

Le Blanc de Blancs

Tostadas
Crisp Fried Tortillas

Tostadas are fried corn tortillas topped with any combination of beans, shredded meat, lettuce, sour cream, and salsa. My children are always reminding me that they prefer ketchup to salsa—so the ketchup is always placed on the table when I serve salsa.

The meat, lettuce, cheese, and salsa can be prepared ahead of time. The beans can also be pre-cooked, and then refried just before serving. The tostadas should be fried several hours ahead of time so that they will drain well.

> *12 corn tortillas*
> *1/2 cup cooking oil or lard*
> *refried beans*
> *chicken, beef, or pork meat—cooked and shredded*
> *lettuce, shredded*
> *tomatoes, chopped (optional)*
> *onions, chopped (optional)*
> *sour cream (optional)*
> *salsa or Mexican canned chiles, sliced*
> *salt*

Fry corn tortillas one at a time in small skillet with heated oil or lard. Fry on medium heat until crisp around the edges, but not too hard. Drain on paper towels.

Garnish each tostada beginning with the refried beans. Add the shredded meat and lettuce; top with whatever you like: sour cream, salsa, or sliced canned chiles. Serve immediately.

Recommended Wines

Dry Gewurztraminer or Le Blanc de Blancs (with chicken)
Sauvignon Blanc (with pork)
Cabernet Sauvignon or Sauvignon Blanc (with beef)

Enchiladas y Salsa a la Paula
Paula's Enchiladas and Sauce

Paula, my husband's mother, has perfected this recipe with years of practice in México. You can buy canned enchilada sauce; or you can buy canned red chili sauce made from Anaheim dry chile pods (adding the seasonings suggested below); or you can buy dry chiles and make Paula's own sauce:

> 8 California dry chiles or
> 4 California chiles and 4 pasilla or ancho chiles or
>   28-ounce can red chili sauce
> 1 teaspoon orégano
> 1 large clove garlic
> 1 medium slice of onion
> pinch of ground cumin seed

Step 1–Making the Sauce

If using fresh chiles, remove the seeds, rinse and soak in hot water for 20 to 30 minutes. (Do not discard the water, as you will use it when blending the chiles.) Place softened chiles in blender jar with water; adding water, if necessary, to cover the chiles. If using canned red chili sauce: place in blender with 1 teaspoon orégano, garlic, slice of onion, and the ground cumin seed.

Blend until smooth. Place sauce in pan and heat for 2 to 4 minutes. Cool for 5 minutes, pour into deep bowl. Salt to taste.

Step 2–Filling and Preparing the Tortillas

For this step you will need:

> 12 corn tortillas
> 2–3 cups chicken, goat, beef, or pork meat,
>   cooked and shredded;
>   or Mexican cheese or Monterey Jack cheese

Maiz y Trijo

1 1/2–3 cups lettuce shredded
  (place in bowl, cover, refrigerate until needed)
1 tomato, sliced
1 onion, sliced
sour cream
salsa
4–5 potatoes
4–5 carrots
1/4 cup cooking oil or lard

Peel and slice carrots into 1/4 or 1/2-inch pieces; then boil in water until tender. Peel and slice potatoes into 1/4 or 1/2-inch thick round circles; then fry in 1/4 cup cooking oil or lard until light brown—add drained carrots to potatoes, cover skillet, and cook on medium low heat for the last 5 minutes of cooking time—turn occasionally to prevent burning. Salt to taste.

Then, while melting 3 tablespoons lard (or cooking oil), preheat a small Teflon skillet on medium heat. Take a tortilla, dip in sauce (salsa), and place in skillet. Heat the tortilla just long enough to soften, but take care not to cook too long, as it may cause the tortilla to fall apart.

Place heated tortilla in a dish. Fill with the desired meat or cheese and roll.

Keep enchiladas warm and serve immediately, 3 to 4 on a plate garnished with lettuce, tomato slices, and onion slices and topped with sour cream and salsa, if desired. Serve fried potatoes and carrots as an accompaniment.

Serves 3–4.

Recommended Wines

Pinot Noir
Zinfandel

Corn and Wheat

Gorditas a la Paula
Paula's Small Corn Tortillas

A **gordita** is a small but thick corn tortilla. Though small in size, preparing gorditas is a big job. The meat must be cooked and shredded. The vegetables must be cut, sliced, and cooked. The salsa must be made.

And finally, the table must be prepared and decorated. This small extra effort will guarantee you a perfect meal worthy of all your work—and well appreciated by all who eat it!

> 1 package masa harina (corn tortilla mix)
> 2–3 pounds flank steak
> 1 clove garlic
> salt
> 1/2 head lettuce
> 4–5 potatoes
> 4–5 carrots
> cooking oil or lard, as needed
> salsa
> sour cream

Mix the masa, according to directions on package, until smooth. Shape dough into balls the size of golf balls; then pat between your fingers and the palms of your hands to shape into plump little tortillas, each fat enough to later hold the filling after being sliced open. Now do one at a time, or whatever you have room for on the griddle. Each should be about 4 inches in diameter.

After placing gorditas on a preheated griddle, cook on medium heat on both sides until done. While still hot, take a knife and slit each gordita to form a pocket (don't slice all the way through—also leave sides closed) to hold the filling. Set the gorditas aside until ready to serve. Cover with foil when cool.

Meanwhile, bring water to boil in a large soup pot (large

enough to cover the meat with plenty of water). When water boils, add meat, 1 clove of garlic, and 1 teaspoon of salt. Bring back to boil on high heat; skim off fat and foam from top of water for 3 to 5 minutes. Cover and simmer until meat is tender. Then drain and shred meat, place in bowl, and cover until ready to use.

Peel and slice carrots into 1/4- or 1/2-inch pieces; boil in water until tender. Peel and slice potatoes into 1/4- or 1/2-inch thick round circles; fry in 1/4 cup light cooking oil or lard until tender—adding carrots to the potatoes the last 5 minutes of cooking time. Salt to taste. Shred lettuce (about 1/2 head); place in bowl, covered, and refrigerate until needed. Now it's time to make the salsa. Tomatíllo or tomato salsa is best. Place in bowl, cover and place on table. Place sour cream on table.

Take gordita and fill with shredded meat about 1/3 to 1/2 full. You should be able to close it up if not filled too much. Fry each gordita on medium heat in 1/2 cup oil. Fry 1/2 to 1 minute on each side. The gordita should be soft, not hard, but a little crunchy. Drain on a paper towel, and then complete the filling with potatoes, carrots, lettuce, and a topping of salsa and sour cream. Serve immediately.

Recommended Wine

 Zinfandel

Tamales a la Martha
Martha's Tamales

There is one thing that the macho Mexican male will do—and that is to help Mexican women make tamales! Could it be because they like to eat them too? Or perhaps they realize all the work and time that must be consumed in making them.

Tamales are made by spreading masa on corn husks, then filling with a delicious savory meat sauce, wrapping, and steaming until done. Because of all the work involved, they are usually made in large quantities and served on special occasions.

I have never met two women who prepare the meat sauce for the filling just the same. The corn masa itself is prepared somewhat all alike. Some prefer to flavor the masa with red chile sauce from the filling. Martha's recipe is my family's favorite; she was the first to show me how to make tamales correctly, and since then I have prepared her tamales with her many times. Martha serves her tamales with rice, salsa, and a green salad made with lettuce, carrots, celery, sliced tomatoes, and sliced avocados.

Step 1–Preparing the Masa

You can prepare the masa yourself with masa harina, a packaged corn tortilla mix. Just follow package directions. Martha and many of my friends buy masa already prepared with all of the ingredients, including the red sauce.

In this recipe you'll need 10 pounds of masa; if making from scratch, you'll need 2 pounds of lard which should be softened so that it can easily be creamed into the masa. After that, you need 1 teaspoon baking powder and then salt to taste. Add some red chile sauce from the meat sauce to color and flavor the masa. Masa from scratch when finished should be smooth and creamy and airy (fluffy).

Step 2–Preparing the Meat

The meat should be lean. The tamales in this recipe call for pork. After cooking until tender, cut out all extra fat (otherwise your tamales are going to taste greasy). Save the broth that the meat cooked in. This can be used in the masa if you are making it from scratch; or it can be used to add extra flavor while steaming the tamales.

> 15 pounds leg of pork (butt)
> 1/2 onion
> 1 garlic clove
> 1 teaspoon salt
> water

Place leg of pork in large pot and cover with water. Bring to boil and boil on high heat for 5 to 7 minutes; keep fat and foam skimmed from top of water. Then add onion, whole garlic, and salt. Cover and reduce heat to simmer and cook until tender. Remove from pot and place in large bowl. Cool, then cut or break up meat into bite-sized pieces. Cover and set aside until sauce is ready.

Step 3–Corn Husks

Buy a supply of dry corn husks (2 or 3 packages) at your local grocery (more and more stores are carrying them). Rinse corn husks under running water to remove silks; then soak in water until soft, 20 to 30 minutes or until ready to use.

Step 4–The Sauce (see next page)

Corn and Wheat

Salsa para Tamales a la Martha
Martha's Tamale Sauce

This sauce may be used with any tamale recipe.

7 California dry chiles
4 pasilla dry chiles
3 garlic cloves

Rinse chiles in cool water, place in pot with garlic, and add enough water to cover all but 1/4 of the chiles. Bring to boil, cover and simmer for 15 to 20 minutes until tender. Then place chiles and water in blender jar to measure approximately 5 cups. Blend on high until smooth.

Strain blended chiles through hand strainer, adding to the prepared meat. Discard the seeds from the strainer. Add meat and sauce to large skillet and cook over medium high; stir when needed to keep from burning. Cook 15 to 20 minutes. Salt to taste. Sauce should be thick; if not, cook until it thickens.

Step 5—Putting the Tamales Together

Remove some corn husks from water and place in a strainer. Put a baking pan under the strainer to catch the water.

Take 1 corn husk. Spread about 2 tablespoons of prepared masa on the bottom 2/3's of the smooth side of the corn husk. Spread masa all the way to the bottom of the large wider end. The smaller 1/3 end should be pointing upward, and it should not be covered with masa. You don't need to spread the masa thick because as it cooks it will thicken.

Place 1 well-rounded tablespoon of meat sauce in the middle of the masa. Take care not to use too much because the sauce will just run out of the corn husks.

Fold sides over each other, covering the meat. (It's like folding a letter into 3 parts to place into an envelope.) Fold the pointed end towards the ends that are overlapping. Stand tamale on that fold in a pan or bowl until you have made enough to steam. (Elena—see next recipe—sometimes rolls her tamales instead of folding them.)

Add to steamer enough broth or water to measure 2 to 3 inches. Place tamales in steamer standing on their folds. Additional layer of tamales may be added.

Cover and place on high heat until you see steam coming out of the pot. Then lower the heat to medium high.

Steam on medium high heat because otherwise they will take forever to cook. I made this mistake several times before Martha and I started cooking them together, when she pointed out the error of my ways! Steaming should take 35 to 45 minutes. The masa will have cooked away from the tips of the corn husks. (When tamales are done, the masa should be lightly firm but not sticky. As tamales cool, they become firm even in the center.)

You may freeze tamales prior to steaming.

Makes 9–10 dozen tamales.

Recommended Wine

Cabernet Sauvignon

Corn and Wheat

Salsa para Tamales a la Elena
Elena's Tamale Filling

This recipe makes about one third the number of tamales as in the previous recipe. After a little practice, you'll be able to develop your own variation.

> 5 pounds pork roast (center loin roast or sirloin roast)
> 6 small dry pasilla chiles
> 12 small dry New Mexico chiles
> 2 whole cloves
> 2 whole black pepper corns
> 3 large or 6 small garlic cloves

Toast chiles on preheated griddle. Then remove seeds and cut off stems. Place in sauce pan—rinse with hot water, then cover chiles with hot water. Soak for 20 to 30 minutes.

Cut pork roast in small chunks; then fry until tender and brown. Drain fat from pan.

In blender process until smooth the soaked chiles, cloves, whole black pepper corns, and garlic. Add to cooked meat. Stir. Cook for 20 minutes. Salt to taste.

Makes 3–4 dozen tamales.

Recommended Wine

Cabernet Sauvignon

SALSAS
Sauces

Mexican cuisine without sauces is inconceivable! On my table, fresh salsa—low in calories and fat—is a must with every meal. Sauces are used in soups, tamales, and for seasoning all of the different meats—beef, chicken, goat, pork, and veal. Enchiladas just wouldn't be enchiladas without the sauce and seasonings.

There are no set rules for making good chile sauces. Since some chiles are hotter than others, you need to experiment with different varieties and combinations to discover just what suits your taste—leaving in all or part of the seeds makes a big difference too!

Sometimes I add fresh or canned chiles to my table, but I'm just as particular with my chiles as I am with my salsas. I use Embasa chiles, canned in México, and available in many stores. There are many good prepared canned sauces that can be used for enchiladas or soups or seasonings for meats. Personally, I have found LAS PALMAS Red Chili Sauce to be one of the finest.

Salsa a la Chávez

Chávez Special Salsa

This unusual blend of chiles, tomatoes, tomatíllos, and garlic is unique because the salsa can be served as a table sauce or cooked with meat to make a savory dish.

> 1 clove garlic, crushed
> 3/4 pound tomatíllos
> 2 yellow or green chiles
> 2-4 ripe firm tomatoes
> 6–10 árbol chiles—the more chiles, the hotter it gets!
> salt

Clean and rinse tomatíllos, tomatoes, and chiles. Place in saucepan, cover with water. Bring to boil, lower heat to medium. Then cook until tomatíllos are tender, but not broken. Drain water.

Add garlic to blender with tomatíllos, chiles, and peeled tomatoes. Process until smooth. Salt to taste. Sauce will keep in refrigerator.

Variation

Cube pork or beef and fry in small amount of light oil until tender. Drain. Add salsa. Cook an additional 3 to 5 minutes. Serve over eggs or with rice, beans, and tortillas.

Mole a la Paula

Paula's Mole

Mole is a classic Mexican sauce usually served over turkey or chicken, but also delicious over pork. I always prepare this sauce a day or two ahead so that the seasonings mellow. Note that New Mexico chiles are much hotter than California chiles, so be sure to use the ones that you prefer.

This recipe can be varied. For example, try adding the mole sauce or powder that is available in Mexican stores or grocery sections. Just add a little at a time, or the spiciness may get ahead of you! Some people prefer adding a few sections of Mexican chocolate which includes almonds and cinnamon.

You can easily double this recipe by using a 28-ounce can of red chili sauce in place of dry chiles.

Mole may also be frozen for later use.

Step 1

> *1–1 1/2 cups chicken broth*
>
> *1/8–1/4 cup cooking oil or lard*
>
> *1/2 cup sesame seeds*
>
> *2 tablespoons peanuts—skinless, salted, and roasted*
>
> *2 tablespoons pumpkin seeds—unshelled, salted, roasted*
>
> *15 whole almonds—fresh shelled*
>
> *2 tablespoons Mexican mixed spices (available in most stores)*
>
> *4 small dry red chiles*
>
> *1/4 medium onion*
>
> *1/2 tomato*

Add all of the above to 1/8 to 1/4 cup heated lard in a large skillet. Fry on medium heat until onion and tomato are tender and seeds and nuts are toasted. Add to blender with 1 cup water and 1 cup chicken broth. Process on high. If blender stops, add an additional 1/2 cup chicken broth and continue processing. When

thoroughly ground, pour sauce through strainer into a mixing bowl. You may need to use a small spoon to stir the sauce in the strainer so liquid will strain through.

Step 2

4 dry California or New Mexico chiles
4 dry ancho or pasilla chiles
1–3 tablespoons cooking oil or lard
hot water
salt

Clean and rinse chiles, removing seeds and stems. Cover with hot water and soak for 20 to 30 minutes. Place chiles in blender with 2 1/2 cups of the water that the chiles were soaked in. Process on high until the chiles are ground. Take 1 to 3 tablespoons of oil or lard and heat in a large skillet. Add blended chiles and cook for 3 minutes.

Now add the strained sauce from Step 1 above. Stir, cook for 10 to 20 minutes until reaching the desired thickness. Stir often to keep from burning. Salt to taste.

Pour over sliced turkey or chicken or even beans and rice.

Sauces

Salsa de Jitomate Fresca
Fresh Tomato Salsa

Salsas can always be made in varying degrees of spiciness and hotness to suit your own taste. This recipe is one that you will find in Mexican restaurants.

>   2 ripe tomatoes, peeled and finely chopped
>   1–3 fresh yellow chiles or serrano green chiles, finely chopped
>   1–2 tablespoons onions, finely chopped
>   cilantro (optional), chopped

Mix all of the above. Salt to taste. May be refrigerated for one day. Makes 1 cup.

Salsa de Chile Rojo
Red Chile Sauce

With California chiles, this is a mild chile sauce. By adding New Mexico chiles, you can make it hotter. Try this sauce served with sour cream over a noodle soup. This sauce can be refrigerated for later use.

>   3 ancho or pasilla (dry chiles)
>   3 California or New Mexico (dry chiles)
>   1/4–1/2 pound tomatíllos
>   1 garlic clove, crushed

Clean and rinse tomatíllos in water. Cover with water and boil until tender. Toast or brown chiles on preheated griddle, medium heat, until soft. Be careful not to burn the dry chiles—just keep turning them until they are soft. Cut off stems and add chiles with seeds to blender. Add tomatíllos and about 1 cup of the water used to boil the tomatíllos (water must still be hot). Add 1 clove of crushed garlic and process until smooth (you may need to add more hot water). Salt to taste.

Makes 1–2 cups depending on size of chiles and tomatíllos.

Salsa de Chile Piquín

Piquín Sauce

Salsa de Chile Piquín is a very hot sauce served from a bowl placed on the table. Try it for breakfast with scrambled eggs, canned cooked pork (fried), and warm tortillas—or serve it for lunch or dinner with meat, refried beans, and warm tortillas. This salsa can be refrigerated.

> *2 medium tomatoes*
> *4 large tomatíllos*
> *4 serrano chiles*
> *1–2 tablespoons dry piquín chiles*
> *1 small clove garlic, crushed*
> *salt*

Clean and rinse tomatíllos; rinse tomatoes and serrano chiles. Place in saucepan with enough water to cover. Bring to boil; then lower heat to medium and cook until tomatíllos are tender (they will turn a lighter shade of green). Remove from heat, drain water, peel tomatoes, and cut off chile stems.

Add garlic to blender jar with tomatoes, tomatíllos, and chiles. Toast piquín chiles lightly on griddle, stirring, and taking care not to burn the chiles—10 to 20 seconds. Then add piquín chiles to blender jar and purée until well blended.

Salt to taste.

Makes 1 cup.

Salsa de Tomatíllo al Gera

Gera's Tomatíllo Sauce

You will find this tomatíllo sauce to be one of the easiest to prepare, and it can be refrigerated for use later. Gera, my brother-in-law, graciously taught me this recipe many years ago, and I have used it often. Mexican men often don aprons to make this salsa for use at outdoor barbecues, so it must be great!

1 clove garlic
1 serrano chile, if desired
4 or more árbol chiles (dry red chiles)
1/2 pound tomatíllos
salt
1 teaspoon chopped cilantro (optional)
1 small slice of onion (optional)

Clean and rinse the tomatíllos and place in saucepan with enough water to cover. Bring to boil and add 1 serrano chile, if desired, and 4 árbol chiles. Reduce heat to medium. Water should be at a low boil. Cook until tender.

Meanwhile, take 1 clove garlic and smash in a **molcajete**, adding a few drops of water to make a paste from the smashed garlic. Add to blender and blend with cooked drained tomatíllos (add the cilantro and onion now, if desired). Process until smooth. Salt to taste.

Serve on tacos, burritos, eggs, or other dishes.

ENSALADAS Y LEGUMBRES
Salads and Vegetables

Many Mexicans cook their vegetables in rice, soups, and sauces. They do not prefer plain vegetables. The vegetable dishes in this section can be served either with other dishes or eaten as a meal in themselves.

Salads in México are eaten with the main meal—not preceding it, as we do in the United States.

Ensalada de Aguacate
Avocado Salad

Avocados are a delight in many Mexican open markets. The variety of sizes and shapes and colors from light to dark green seems endless. This recipe is good with any of them.

2 medium ripe but firm avocados
2 medium ripe but firm tomatoes
1/2 small onion, minced
2–4 small green or yellow chiles—the more the hotter!
salt to taste

Peel and chop tomatoes. Place in salad bowl with minced onion. Peel and chop avocados into 1/2 to 1-inch cubes. Put the avocado pits into the salad bowl, as this will help prevent the avocado from turning brown so quickly (use this hint when storing half an avocado in your refrigerator too—replace the pit in the unused half).

Rinse and chop, finely, the chile peppers. Combine with the salad, add salt, and toss lightly to keep from smashing the tomatoes and avocados.

Cover and chill, if desired, or serve at once. A welcome complement to barbecued meat, chicken, rice, or refried beans.

Serves 2–4.

Ensalada de Enchilada
Enchilada Salad

Prepare individual salads. The chicken in this recipe is seasoned with Paula's enchilada sauce (see page 72). The shredded chicken should be dry before seasoning. Use enchilada sauce sparingly. For extra flavor, dip the tortillas in sauce before frying lightly.

> *4 corn tortillas*
> *2 cups shredded lettuce*
> *2–3 cups shredded chicken*
> *sliced tomatoes (optional)*
> *salsa*
> *sour cream*
> *enchilada sauce*
> *light cooking oil*

Boil chicken in water, skimming off foam and fat from the boiling liquid before covering and simmering until tender. Drain and shred. Add enough enchilada sauce to season meat. Keep warm.

Fry each corn tortilla lightly on both sides. Drain and place on plates. Top with shredded chicken and shredded lettuce and serve. Toppings of tomatoes, sour cream, and salsa may be added at the table.

Serve as a light meal.

Recommended Wines

Johannisberg Riesling
Semillon

Ensalada a la estilo Mama
Mama's Macaroni Salad

J uan, my dearest brother–in–law (mi guerido cuña-dito), will tell you that this salad is always his favorite; it may be made in the morning for the evening meal, or for serving the next day—just as we do, it improves with age!

1 pound salad macaroni
5 quarts water
4 eggs, boiled and finely chopped
1 egg, boiled and sliced for garnish
3 medium tomatoes (about 3 inches in diameter)
1 cup mayonnaise
1 teaspoon salt
1/2 cup onion, minced
1/2 cup celery, minced
1/2 teaspoon paprika

and, if you like, for a different taste

a few sliced or chopped pickled peppers

Bring 5 quarts water to boil in a large pot. Add macaroni and stir slowly for 1 to 2 minutes to prevent sticking. Lower heat slightly to prevent boiling over (a spoonful of cooking oil will also help prevent boilover). Stir occasionally and cook according to directions on the package (not too chewy or mushy). Then rinse macaroni with cold water and let stand in a pot of cold water for 5 or 10 minutes before draining.

Place in large bowl and mix in onions, celery, and 4 eggs. Add 1 cup mayonnaise. Mix well again. Add salt and paprika and tomatoes; tossing thoroughly. Place in a serving bowl, garnish with 1 sliced egg, and sprinkle lightly with paprika. Cover bowl and chill for 3 hours or overnight before serving.

Serves 4.

Salads and Vegetables

Ensalada de Papa
Potato Salad

Everyone has a favorite potato salad. By changing ingredients, you can use this one, my favorite, as the basis for your own special creation. Some like it hot! Some like it cold! But it won't get nine days old!

6 medium potatoes, boiled with skin until tender

4 medium eggs, hard boiled

1/2 cup white or red onion, finely chopped

4 teaspoons mustard

2 tablespoons white distilled vinegar—the more you add the tangier it gets!

3/4 cup mayonnaise

1/8 teaspoon paprika

salt to taste

and, if you like, for a different taste

a few sliced or chopped pickled peppers

Boil potatoes, covered with water, in pan until tender.

Boil eggs 10 minutes. Pour off hot water, replace with cold, and set eggs aside.

Take potatoes, remove skin, and cut into 2-inch chunks. Place in large mixing bowl. Remove shells from boiled eggs, and rinse. Chop eggs finely; add to cut potatoes in bowl. Add onions, mayonnaise, mustard and mix. Add vinegar and paprika. Salt to taste. Mix.

Place salad in serving bowl, then sprinkle lightly with paprika. Garnish with an extra boiled egg, sliced. Cover and refrigerate or serve warm.

Serves 4.

Coliflor
Cauliflower

Cauliflower is one of the most popular Mexican vegetables.

1 head cauliflower
2 eggs
salt
1/2 cup shortening, cooking oil or lard

Cut cauliflower into flowerets. Rinse and boil in water until fork tender. Drain and cool.

Meanwhile, beat 2 egg whites until firm; then add the egg yokes and salt and beat lightly. Heat 1/2 cup oil or lard in skillet. Dip flowerets in egg mixture (by adding 1 tablespoon of flour to the egg mixture before dipping vegetables, the mixture will stay firmer longer) and fry on medium heat until golden brown on all sides. Drain on paper towels. Serve with or without Salsa de Jitomate (see page 99).

Papas en Salsa
Potatoes in Hot Sauce

4–5 Idaho potatoes

1 medium onion

2–4 tablespoons shortening, lard, or cooking oil

8–ounce can tomato sauce, Mexican style
  or 8 ounces of your own salsa

2–4 cups water

Peel and rinse 4 to 5 potatoes; cut into round slices. Brown, on medium heat, in 2 to 4 tablespoons of lard for about 2 to 3 minutes. Cut onions into ringlets and toss gently with potatoes.

Cook 5 minutes. Add the Mexican style tomato sauce, or salsa, and enough water to cover potatoes and onions. Bring to boil and simmer, covered, until potatoes are fork tender. Salt to taste.

Serve in shallow soup bowls with warm tortillas. Serve at lunch as a soup or vegetable or as the main dinner dish.

Serves 4 generously.

Tortas de Papa
Little Potato Cakes

This recipe has three variations: Serve any of these recipes with beans, rice, meat, fresh salsa, and warm tortillas. Can be served for breakfast, lunch, or dinner.

3–4 medium sized potatoes
salt
2 eggs
1/2 cup light cooking oil or lard

Recipe 1

Boil 3 to 4 medium sized potatoes until tender. Drain and cool. Peel and mash and salt to taste. Form into 2 x 3-inch patties 1/2 to 3/4-inches thick. Beat 2 egg whites until firm; add egg yolks, salt lightly and beat until blended. Dip potato patties, one at a time, into egg mixture until thoroughly coated and fry in 1/2 cup heated oil or lard until golden brown on both sides. Drain on paper towel. Can be served in Salsa de Jitomate (see page 99).

Recipe 2

After boiling and peeling, mash and salt potatoes to taste. Add 2 eggs. Beat lightly with mixer or by hand until blended. Pour, one by one, to make patties 1 1/2 to 2-inches in diameter into heated oil or lard and fry until golden brown. Serve with or without Salsa de Jitomate.

Recipe 3

After potatoes are boiled and peeled, grate potatoes with grater, salt, form into patties. Fry in oil or lard until golden brown and crisp on both sides. Drain.

Serves 4.

Chiles Rellenos
Stuffed Chiles

Chiles Rellenos are made with fresh green pasilla or Anaheim chiles that are stuffed with either meat or cheese, then served either with or without Salsa de Jitomate (see page 99). There are cheeses available now with different seasonings, such as a chile Monterey Jack that will add hotness to the stuffed chiles.

4 fresh green pasilla or Anaheim chiles
1 pound Monterey Jack cheese (cut into 1 x 1/2-inch slices)
2 eggs
1 tablespoon flour (optional)
salt
1/2 cup light cooking oil or lard

Rinse and dry chiles. Toast chiles on an open fire or griddle. Cool. Scrape the dark toasted chiles with a dull knife. Slit the chiles on one side in order to fill. When chiles are filled, beat two egg whites until firm; then add the egg yokes and salt and beat lightly until blended. At this time, you can fold the flour into the egg mixture, or you can roll the chiles in the flour; then dip the chiles in the egg mixture and fry in hot oil until golden brown. Remember, the flour is not necessary. After frying, drain the chiles on paper towels.

Serve in a shallow soup bowl with Salsa de Jitomate and beans or rice, or both, on the side of the same dish. Serve with warm tortillas for lunch or dinner.

Serves 2–4.

Recommended Wines

Chardonnay
Johannisberg Riesling

Ensaladas y Legumbres

Salsa de Jitomate
Light Tomato Sauce

This sauce is used with potato cakes and chile rellenos. Pour sauce into individual shallow soup bowls. Place chile rellenos and potato cakes on top. Serve with rice or beans on the side.

1 cup tomatoes, blended, or 1 cup tomato sauce
1/2 medium onion, cut in ringlets
2–3 tablespoons light cooking oil or lard
2–3 cups water
1–2 pinches ground cumin seed (optional)

Heat oil or lard in skillet. Add onion and fry lightly. Stir often, until almost tender, not browning onions. Add tomatoes and water and bring to boil. Salt to taste, and add a pinch or two of ground cumin seed, if desired. Simmer for 5 minutes.

Chiles Rellenos
a la Comadre Celia

Comadre Celia's Stuffed Chiles

Here is an excellent recipe for stuffed chiles.

6 dry pasilla chiles
3 medium potatoes
1 1/2 ounces or more grated Parmesan cheese
flour
2 eggs

Split pasilla chiles on side; remove seeds. Rinse inside and outside and dry with paper towel. Open slightly, and fill.

Egg Batter

Beat 2 egg whites until firm. Add egg yolks and beat lightly until blended. Add salt if desired.

Filling

Take potatoes cooked whole, in their skins, in boiling water. Peel and mash. Then add desired amount of cheese and mix with potatoes. Stuff into pasilla chiles, but don't overfill. Roll in flour, dip in egg batter, and fry until golden brown on all sides.

Serve with rice, refried beans, salsa, and tortillas for lunch or dinner.

Serves 3–6.

Frijoles
Beans

A pot of freshly cooked beans on the stove is the hallmark of the Mexican home. Beans—whether served freshly cooked or refried for serving with soups, meats and sauces, tostadas, burritos, or tacos—are an essential part of any Mexican meal. Beans are versatile, easy to prepare, and good to eat. Add a fresh sprig of epazote to the beans during the last half-hour of cooking—for flavoring, and to help remove some of the gas from the beans.

Basic Recipe

> *1 pound pinto, pink, or kidney beans*
> *12–14 cups water*
> *1 sprig fresh epazote (optional)*

Sort and rinse beans, add cold water to pan, bring to boil. Follow instructions on bean package or boil slowly until tender— about 4 hours. Or bring to boil, then cover and simmer for 1 hour, then pressure cook for 20 minutes. Add salt when finished.

Refried Beans

Heat 2 to 4 tablespoons cooking oil or lard in skillet, and fry a slice of onion for 2 minutes. Remove and discard onion. Add cooked beans to frying pan with very little liquid; then mash and stir. Cook until dry, stirring when needed. May also be fried until crisp.

Tunas
Prickly Pears

Prickly pears are the purple-red fruit of the cactus **Opuntia tuna**. (The yellow-fruited **Opuntia Ficus-Indica** is also well known.) Both are eaten raw or stewed with other fruit, such as lemon or pineapple. In California, when ripe, large clumps of red prickly pears, are often seen growing on tall green cactus plants.

With over 150 members in the **Opuntia** genus, they are cool and refreshing and reputed to have medicinal qualities.

Cut fruit from plant very carefully. Brush or rub spines away. Then rinse and peel. Boil until tender. Add lemon juice (some like hot sauce too), and serve.

Nopales
Cactus Leaves

Nopales, the leaves of the **Optunia tuna** cactus is available in stores already diced and cooked, either in jars or in cans. Just drain well and mix with your favorite red chili sauce.

If you prefer it fresh, handle the cactus leaves with care. Use only the young, tender leaves (trim the base). Remove needles, and trim all sides. Peel, wash, dice, and boil in water until tender, approximately 10 to 20 minutes. Drain and rinse thoroughly in cold water.

About two cups of cooked leaves, together with 2 or 3 tablespoons olive oil, will make a nice salad. Or add to meat and eggs for an exotic breakfast dish.

BEBIDAS Y POSTRES
Beverages And Desserts

Other than beer, wine, tequila, and hard liquor, there are a number of beverages available in México. **Ponche**, or punch, for example, is made from fruit juices, sugar, and other flavorings. **Atole**, made with masa, sugar, and flavorings is available premade in packages—just add water.

Chocolate is a well known traditional Mexican drink. One popular brand comes in round, hard cakes. Prepare by adding milk and heating until the chocolate melts, then beating with a **molinillo** (or in a blender) until the chocolate foams.

I have also seen my husband's mother make a cinnamon tea for cold mornings or nights. Fill a pot with 8 to 12 cups of water; add 1 or 2 sticks of cinnamon, breaking them up, and bring the water to a boil. Cover and simmer on low heat until the tea attains the desired color. Hard liquor can be added to the tea, along with sugar.

Beer has been brewed in México for almost 500 years, and of course I favor Mexican beer with Mexican food; of the many excellent Mexican beers available, my personal preference is for the heavier, dark varieties.

México is a land of venerable vineyards, some of the newest being in Baja California. So it is natural to serve wine with Mexican food, a tradition that is being revived in California in some of the finest Mexican restaurants. In our home, we serve sparkling wine with Mexican food on special occasions such as New Year's Eve—when we toast out the old, toast in the new, before sitting down to dinner. My favorites with Mexican food are Semillon and Chardonnay Reserve, but many people prefer a White Zinfandel.

The desserts in this section have been given the "empty plate" test with our friends and relatives. Some are purely Mexican, some American with a Mexican touch; some, especially the Jell-O, are popular with children.

Recommended Wines with Desserts

 Brut Sparkling Wine
Arroyo Seco Riesling

Bebidas y Postres

Blue Moon Margaritas

Anyone can make a margarita—and everyone does! They are great party favorites. But the **Blue Moon Margarita** is for romantic evenings (or for use when you're serving those blue corn flour chips). Prepare with 3 parts tequila to 1 part blue curacao (substitute triple sec if you don't like blue!). Add 2 parts lemon juice to mixture.

Rub the rim of the glass with the lemon rind, then dip the rim in salt. Shake the margarita with crushed ice and strain into a glass.

Enjoy!

Sangria

Sangria, American style, is the wine of your choice mixed with fruit juice. Make it any way you like, in any proportions that you like. Sweeten to taste, and add crushed ice, if desired. For a more solid beverage, or sangrilla, combine the sangria with mashed fruit, such as melons, peaches, pears, oranges, strawberries.

Let your taste buds be your guide!

Desayuno con Plátano
Banana Breakfast

In México, the variety of bananas which are available is truly marvelous. Here in the United States, we get one kind—but soon, I'm told, we'll have many others to choose from in our stores.

> 1–1 1/2 cups milk
> 1 egg
> 2 teaspoons sugar (optional)
> 1 banana
> 1 or 2 dashes ground cinnamon

Mix in blender on high for 30 seconds. Pour into glass. Serves 1.

Arroz con Leche
Rice Pudding

Everyone has a favorite rice pudding recipe, but the cinnamon gives this one a special Mexican flavor.

> 1 cup uncooked long grain white rice
> 3 cups water
> 3–4 sticks cinnamon
> 2 eggs, beaten (optional)
> 1/2–3/4 cup sugar
> 2 cups milk (lowfat can be used)
> 1/4 cup raisins (optional)

Rinse rice three times in cold water. Then place water, rice, and cinnamon in sauce pan. Bring to boil. Cover and simmer until water is absorbed. Remove from heat and allow to cool.

Then, in a bowl, mix milk, sugar, beaten eggs and raisins. Add cooled rice to mixture. Stir and bring to a low boil over medium heat. Then turn heat down to a simmer. Stir often. Cook about 10 minutes or until thick (it will thicken more as it cools).

Remove the cinnamon sticks. Serve warm or cold.

Serves 4–6.

Camotes a la Mexicana
Sweet Potatoes Mexican Style

Here are potatoes sweet enough for a dessert.

3–4 sweet potatoes
1 stick cinnamon
8 ounces panocha (Mexican brown sugar)

Take sweet potatoes, cut off ends. Rinse in water, place loosely in large deep pot. Cover with water to depth of half the sweet potatoes. Add the cinnamon stick and the panocha; bring to a boil. The panocha will melt with the heat, so there is no need to cut it up. Cover and simmer until potatoes are tender. The sauce should be thick when ready.

Serve the sweet potatoes as they are, or place in a bowl with cold or warm milk and peel the potatoes as you eat.

Good for breakfast, or for an after lunch or dinner dessert.
Serves 2–4.

Capirotada
Bread Pudding

Here is a bread pudding made with leftover pound cake. Some people spoon Kahlua over the top.

2 cups leftover pound cake, cubed and packed
1 cup milk
1/4 teaspoon ground cinnamon
1 small pinch nutmeg
1 small pinch cloves
2 eggs, beaten
1/3 cup brown sugar

Combine beaten eggs, milk, brown sugar, cinnamon, nutmeg, and cloves. Mix with wire whip. Pour over cubed and packed pound cake. Mix gently.

Pour into buttered casserole dish. Bake in preheated oven at 375 degrees for 15 minutes or until knife inserted comes out clean. Serve warm or cold.

Serves 4.

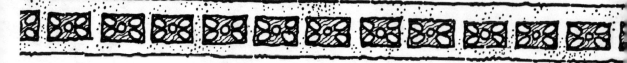

Flan
Custard

This light and smooth dessert is a Mexican classic; here again, if you like, spoon on Kahlua before serving (garnish with mint sprigs).

 4 eggs
 2 cups half and half, or milk
 1/2 teaspoon vanilla extract
 1/4 cup sugar
 1/8–1/4 cup almonds, walnuts, or coconut pieces
 1/4 cup sugar (for the caramel)
 1/4–1/2 cup Kahlua (optional)
 pinch of salt
 cinnamon

Heat sugar for caramel in Teflon pan, stirring constantly until the sugar melts and turns a golden color. Pour into a 1 quart glass baking dish, tipping dish around until it is coated with caramel. Don't worry if caramel doesn't cover bottom of mold because it will spread during cooking.

Mix in a blender or in a bowl with a mixer, the eggs, milk, sugar, salt, vanilla, nuts, and Kahlua (if desired). Blend or mix well. Remove any foam because it causes bubbles to form in the custard. Pour mixture into the caramel covered baking dish. Sprinkle lightly with cinnamon.

Place baking dish in a pan of water so that water covers the bottom half of the baking dish. Bake covered in preheated 350 degree oven for 45 minutes to 1 hour. Check by inserting clean knife into center of custard. Knife comes out clean if done. Chill.

Serves 4–6.

Fruta Tropicana con Queso
Tropical Fruit Plate with Cheese

Fresh fruit will bring color to your table and joy to your palate!

Fresh fruit of your choice:
>bananas, guava, limes, mangoes, oranges, pineapple, strawberries, or whatever is in season.

Mexican or other cheeses of your choice:
>Jarlsberg, Monterey Jack or Longhorn cheddar; sliced or cubed on toothpicks.

Arrange the fruit and cheese in a colorful pattern on a white plate for maximum contrast. For example, alternate the colors around the plate, placing the cheese together on either half of the plate; or, alternate the cheeses and the fruit around the plate. Garnish with fresh mint sprigs.

Galletas
Filled Cookies

These filled cookies are like fruit bars; fill them with anything from marmalade to jam; or use the filling recipe below.

3 1/2 cups all-purpose, presifted flour
3 teaspoons baking power
1/2 teaspoon salt
1 cup sugar
1/2 cup butter
1 egg
1/2 cup milk
1 teaspoon vanilla

Mix all the dry ingredients thoroughly, then add remaining ingredients. Roll until thin on a lightly floured doughboard. Using a round cookie cutter, cut out and place cookies on a greased cookie sheet. Use a small spoon to make a slight indentation in each to help provide for the filling.

Place a teaspoon of filling in the indentation on each cookie. Do not allow the filling to spread as far as the edges of the cookies. Place another cookie on top; then press down the edges to secure the filling.

Bake in a moderately hot oven, 350 to 375 degrees, for 10 to 12 minutes or until cookies are light brown.

Filling

1/2 cup sugar
1 tablespoon all-purpose flour, presifted
1 cup chopped raisins, dates, or apricots
1/2 cup water

Mix the sugar and flour together, then add the 1/2 cup water. Add 1 cup of either chopped raisins, dates, or apricots. Cook until thick, stirring constantly.

Makes 2–3 dozen cookies.

Pastel de Sandra Maine

Sandra Maine's Pound Cake

My dear and long time friend, Sandy, and I had fun testing this favorite recipe of hers. Mexicans eat this delightful dessert on special occasions.

If you want something extra special, Sandy suggests trying this by adding strawberries and whipped cream to the finished product.

> *2 cups all-purpose flour, presifted*
> *2 sticks butter (1/2 pound), at room temperature*
> *5 eggs at room temperature*
> *1/8 teaspoon salt*
> *2 cups sugar*
> *2 teaspoons vanilla*

Beat butter in a mixer for 1 to 2 minutes. Add sugar to the butter. Cream together for an additional 2 minutes. Break 5 eggs into a separate bowl; slowly add one egg at a time to the butter and sugar mixture. Mix well with mixer for 2 more minutes. Then add vanilla and salt; mix for 1 minute, then add flour. Blend for 3 minutes.

Spray angel food cake pan with no-stick corn oil cooking spray, or oil and flour pan. Use two loaf pans, if desired. Pour batter into pan and bake in preheated oven at 325 degrees for 45 minutes to 1 hour. (Check 10 minutes before time to take out, as ovens will vary.) Insert toothpick into cake—if toothpick comes out clean, then cake is done. Shake pan to loosen. Cool cake for 10 to 15 minutes before removing from pan.

Cake will be a light golden brown with a crisp, crunchy top. Can be served hot or cold. Excellent for buffets, picnics, and outdoor barbecues.

Serves 6–8.

Elegante Pastel de Limon
a la Abuela

Grandmother's Elegant Lemon Cake

This is a favorite dessert in our family. I've used it more often than any other, both for indoor meals and outdoor barbecues. What makes this recipe different from a traditional lemon cake is the addition of Jell-O and the extra eggs. The brand of cake mix is important too—each will give a different result.

1 box lemon cake mix
1 small box Jell-O brand gelatin, lemon flavor
3/4 cup cooking oil
4 eggs
2 tablespoons freshly squeezed lemon juice
1 cup boiling water

In a large mixing bowl, add 1 cup boiling water to gelatin. Stir until dissolved. Then add lemon juice, oil, eggs, and the cake mix. I prefer to use a glass pan greased with shortening or lard as this cake burns easily. Bake according to directions on cake mix box, but check 10 minutes ahead of projected completion.

It's not necessary to frost this cake, but my grandmother used to put on a very light frosting immediately after taking the cake from the oven. This is made by melting 3 to 4 tablespoons butter, then adding 2 tablespoons fresh lemon juice, and 3/4 cup powdered sugar. Beat with mixer. This melts into the hot cake, leaving a very light, thin, and delicious frosting.

Serves 10.

Pan de Nues
Pecan or Pine Nut Bread

Without my friend Martha, learning Mexican cooking would have been a harder task. This easy to make pecan or pine nut bread recipe is Martha's.

14 ounces sweetened condensed milk
1/2 teaspoon baking powder
3/4 cup all-purpose flour, presifted
1/2 cup water
1/4–1/3 cup sugar
1/2 teaspoon vanilla
1 cup raw pecan pieces
    or
1/2 cup pecan pieces and 1/2 cup pine nuts

Place all of the above ingredients in a blender jar and process on low speed. Stop and stir with spatula when necessary. Process on lower speeds only until well mixed. Pour into presprayed or buttered 12 x 6 inch glass pan. Bake cake in oven preheated to 375 degrees for 30 minutes or until done. Cake is done when clean knife inserted into center of bread comes out clean. Cool in pan. Serve warm or cold.
    Serves 4–6.

Polvorones
Tea Cakes

2 cups all-purpose flour, presifted
3 teaspoons baking powder
1/2 cup sugar
1 cup chopped nuts
1 tablespoon butter
1 egg
1 cup milk

Mix the butter and sugar together; add the beaten egg. Then blend in the flour, baking powder and milk.

When all ingredients have been mixed, stir in chopped nuts. Pour mixture into greased muffin pan and bake at 350 to 400 degrees for 20 to 25 minutes. If a toothpick inserted into the center of the cake comes out clean, the cake is done.

Before serving, sprinkle with sugar and cinnamon; or with maple syrup and chopped nuts.

Serve warm.

Makes 12 cakes.

Postre de Empanadas
Dessert Turnovers

Last-minute visitors and nothing on hand to serve? Try these easily made fruit-filled turnovers. You can make them even faster by keeping a package or two of unbaked crescent rolls on hand. All you do is fill, seal, roll, and bake.

While you'll find **Empanadas** and **Empanaditas** elsewhere in this book, you'll notice that I've added sugar to the dough for this recipe

> *1 cup all-purpose flour, presifted and*
> *1/2 teaspoon baking powder*
> > *or 1 cup self-rising flour*
>
> *2 tablespoons sugar*
>
> *1/2 teaspoon salt*
>
> *1/4 cup shortening, or lard*
>
> *3-4 tablespoons ice water*
>
> *filling of your choice*

Into a mixing bowl sift together the dry ingredients. Then add shortening. With pastry blender or fingers, blend shortening together with the flour. Add just enough ice water for the dough to hold together.

Divide dough into 6 pieces. Roll out each piece on a floured board to make a round shape about 4 inches in diameter. Put in a spoonful of your favorite filling. Fold over and seal the edges. Deep fry in hot oil or bake at 375–400 degrees for 10 to 15 minutes, or until light golden brown. Dust with sugar and cinnamon. For an added touch serve with coffee.

Serves 6.

Suggested Dessert Fillings

- ☐ Fruit preserves or jams
- ☐ Mashed and cooked pumpkin with sugar
- ☐ Canned fruit without liquid
- ☐ Crushed pineapple
- ☐ Apples, cinnamon, and sugar

Buñuelos
Mexican Doughnuts

Buñuelos are somewhat like little square puffed up pillows. They can be sprinkled with sugar and cinnamon or served with canned caramel (a favorite Mexican confection, manufactured in Celaya as well as elsewhere).

2 cups all-purpose flour, presifted
1 1/2 teaspoons baking powder
1/4 teaspoon salt
1/4 cup sugar
2 tablespoons shortening or lard
3/4 cup cold water

Sift all dry ingredients together. Then cut in the shortening or lard. Add cold water slowly so as to form a pastry dough. Knead for 2 to 3 minutes. Place in covered bowl in refrigerator for 15 to 20 minutes. Then place dough on floured board and roll out 1/4 inch thick. Cut into 2 inch or 3 inch squares and drop into 350 to 375 degree oil. Press lightly with fork to make them puff up.

Fry until a light golden brown on both sides. Drain on paper towels and sprinkle with sugar and cinnamon or spoon on caramel. Serve warm.

Makes 1 or 2 dozen, depending on the size of the squares.

Rompope con Gelatina
Jell-O with Eggnog

Yes, it's only Jell-O—but....

Once upon a time I was invited to a special holiday dinner. After the meal, several of the children, to my surprise, immediately cleared away the dishes and plates.

Then they all sat down, brown eyes sparkling in eager anticipation of the dessert, Jell-O with eggnog in tall glasses! This happens regularly after one of Paula's dinners.

Paula's recipe doesn't include the fruit or coconut, but the older children and adults may enjoy the added touch.

> *Jell-O, to equal 36 ounces*
> *1/2–1 cup can fruit cocktail, if desired*
> > *or*
> *cherries with cherry Jell-O, strawberries with strawberry*
> > *Jell-O, etc.*
> > *or*
> *add shredded coconut*

Have ready a medium to large mixing bowl. Put required amount of water, plus an extra 1 1/2 cups water, in a pot; bring water to boil. Quickly measure out the 1 1/2 cups extra boiling water, and pour into mixing bowl to heat the bowl for 30 seconds to 1 minute (this prevents a small amount of the dry Jell-O from solidifying on the bottom of the bowl). Reduce heat on remaining water so it won't boil away. Remove water used to heat the bowl; immediately pour in remainder of boiling water. Add Jell-O to boiling water in the bowl. Stir thoroughly until Jell-O is completely dissolved. Then add an equal amount of chilled water to the bowl, stir to mix.

Pour into six 12-ounce glasses, each a little over half full. Place glasses in refrigerator to thicken. When partially set, add fruit or coconut, if desired; stir in gently. Replace glasses in refrigerator to set.

Before serving, pour eggnog over the top of Jell-O in each glass, and serve. You may also use small 6 to 8 ounce dessert dishes to add a special touch of elegance for the adults.

Serves 6.

Sample Menus

Breakfast Menu

Fresh-squeezed Orange Juice
Arturo's Eggs
Pork with Tomatoes
Refried Beans
Tortillas
Coffee or Hot Chocolate

Lunch Menu

Salsa and Chips
Stuffed Chiles
Rice — Beans
Lettuce with a Wedge of Tomato
Salsa — Tortillas
Beer

Special Lunch or Dinner Menu

Shrimp Appetizer — Chips
Grilled Meat
Avocado Salad — Potato Salad
Refried Beans — Mexican Rice
Tortillas — Salsa
Beer or Wine or Tequila

Dinner Menu

Sour Cream Dip with Jalapeños or Tomato Salsa and Chips
Meat in Red Chile Sauce
Mexican Rice — Refried Beans

Fresh Tomato Salsa or Mexican Canned Chiles
Tortillas
Cabernet Sauvignon or Beer

Dinner Menu

Paula's Enchiladas
Carrots and Potatoes
Lettuce — Sour Cream
Tomato Salsa or Gera's Tomatíllo Salsa
Tortillas
Jell-O with Eggnog
Pinot Noir or Zinfandel or Beer

Holiday Menu — Christmas or New Year's

Guacamole — Chips
Turkey — Mole
Rice — Beans
Tamales
Tomato Salsa — Tortillas
Pecan or Pine Nut Bread — Buñuelos
Sangria — Atole

Buffet Menu

Mother's Taco Buffet
Sandra's Pound Cake
Sliced Strawberries — Whipped Cream
White Zinfandel or Beer